Schooling Beyond Measure

ALSO BY ALFIE KOHN

No Contest: The Case Against Competition (1986)

The Brighter Side of Human Nature:
Altruism and Empathy in Everyday Life (1990)

You Know What They Say . . . : The Truth About Popular Beliefs (1990)

Punished by Rewards: The Trouble with Gold Stars, Incentive Plans, A's,
Praise, and Other Bribes (1993)

Beyond Discipline: From Compliance to Community (1996)

Education, Inc.: Turning Learning into a Business [editor] (1997)

What to Look for in a Classroom . . . and Other Essays (1998)

The Schools Our Children Deserve: Moving Beyond Traditional Classrooms and
"Tougher Standards" (1999)

The Case Against Standardized Testing:
Raising the Scores, Ruining the Schools (2000)

What Does It Mean to Be Well Educated?
And More Essays on Standards, Grading, and Other Follies (2004)

Unconditional Parenting:
Moving from Rewards and Punishments to Love and Reason (2005)

The Homework Myth: Why Our Kids Get Too Much of a Bad Thing (2006)

Feel-Bad Education:
And Other Contrarian Essays on Children and Schooling (2011)

The Myth of the Spoiled Child:
Challenging the Conventional Wisdom About Children and Parenting (2014)

Schooling Beyond Measure

& OTHER **UNORTHODOX ESSAYS** ABOUT EDUCATION

ALFIE KOHN

HEINEMANN
Portsmouth, NH

Heinemann
361 Hanover Street
Portsmouth, NH 03801–3912
www.heinemann.com

Offices and agents throughout the world

Cataloging-in-Publication Data is on file at the Library of Congress.

ISBN: 978-0-325-07440-5

Acquisitions Editor: Thomas Newkirk
Production Editor: Patty Adams
Cover and Interior Designs: Suzanne Heiser
Typesetter: Eric Rosenbloom, Kirby Mountain Composition
Manufacturing: Steve Bernier

Printed in the United States of America on acid-free paper
19 18 17 16 15   VP   1 2 3 4 5

CONTENTS

PART 1

How School Reform

Undermines Education

CHAPTER 1

"We're Number Umpteenth!"
The Myth of Lagging U.S. Schools

Beliefs that are debatable or even patently false may be repeated so often that at some point they come to be accepted as fact. We seem to have crossed that threshold with the claim that U.S. schools are significantly worse than those in most other countries. Sometimes the person who parrots this line will even insert a number — "We're only ____th in the world, you know!" — although, not surprisingly, the number changes with each retelling.

The assertion that our students compare unfavorably to those in other countries has long been heard from politicians and corporate executives whose goal is to justify various "get tough" reforms: high-stakes testing, a nationalized curriculum (see under: Common Core "State" Standards), more homework, a longer school day or year, and so on. But by now the premise is apt to be casually repeated by just about everyone — including educators, I'm sorry to say — and in the service of a wide range of prescriptions and agendas. Just recently I've seen it on a petition to promote teaching the "whole child" (which I declined to sign for that reason), in a documentary arguing for more thoughtful math instruction, and in an article by the progressive journalist Barbara Ehrenreich.

Unsurprisingly, this misconception has filtered out to the general public. According to a brand-new poll, a plurality of Americans — and a majority of college graduates! — believe (incorrectly) that American fifteen-year-olds are

"We're Number Umpteenth!": The Myth of Lagging U.S. Schools" was originally published as a blog post on May 3, 2013.

at the bottom when their scores on tests of science knowledge are compared to those of students in other developed countries.[1]

A dedicated group of educational experts has been challenging this canard over the years, but their writings rarely appear in popular publications, and each typically focuses on just one of the many problems with the claim. Here, then, is a concise overview of the multiple responses you might offer the next time you hear someone declare that American kids come up short. (First, though, I'd suggest politely inquiring as to the evidence for his or her statement. The wholly unsatisfactory reply you're likely to receive may constitute a rebuttal in its own right.)

1. Even taking the numbers at face value, the U.S. fares reasonably well. Results will vary depending on subject matter, age, which test is being used, and which year's results are being reported. It's possible to cherry-pick scores to make just about any country look especially good or bad. The U.S. looks considerably better when we focus on younger students, for example — so, not surprisingly, it's the high school numbers that tend to be cited most often. (When someone reduces all student performance to a single number, you can bet it's the one that casts our schools in the worst possible light.)

But even with older students, there may be less to the claim than meets the eye. As an article in *Scientific American* noted a few years back, most countries' science scores were actually pretty similar.[2] That's worth keeping in mind whenever a new batch of numbers is released. If there's little (or even no) statistically significant difference among, say, the nations placing third through ninth, it would be irresponsible to cite those rankings as if they were meaningful.

Overall, when a pair of researchers carefully reviewed half a dozen different international achievement surveys conducted from 1991 to 2001, they found that "U.S. students have generally performed *above average* in comparisons with students in other industrialized nations."[3] And that still seems to be the case with the most recent data, which include math and science scores for grade 4, grade 8, and age fifteen, as well as reading scores for grade 4 and age fifteen. Of the eight results, the U.S. scored above average in five, average in two, and below average in one.[4] Not exactly the dire picture that's typically painted.

2. What do we really learn from standardized tests? While there are differences in quality between the most commonly used tests (e.g., PISA, TIMSS), the fact is that *any* one-shot, pencil-and-paper standardized test — particularly one whose questions are multiple-choice — offers a deeply flawed indicator of learning as compared with authentic classroom-based assessments.[5] One of them taps students' skill at taking standardized tests, which is a skill unto itself; the other taps what students have learned and what sense they make of, and what they can do with, what they've learned. One is a summary statistic labeled "student achievement"; the other is an account of *students' achievements*. Anyone who cites the results of a test is obliged to defend the construction of the test itself, to show that the results are not only statistically valid but meaningful. Needless to say, very few people who say something like "the U.S. is below average in math" have any idea how math proficiency has been measured.

3. Are we comparing apples to watermelons? Even if the tests were good measures of important intellectual proficiencies, the students being tested in different countries aren't always comparable. As scholars Iris Rotberg and the late Gerald Bracey have pointed out for years, some countries test groups of students who are unrepresentative with respect to age, family income, or number of years spent studying science and math. The older, richer, and more academically selective a cohort of students in a given country, the better that country is going to look in international comparisons.[6]

4. Rich American kids do fine; poor American kids don't. It's ridiculous to offer a summary statistic for all children at a given grade level in light of the enormous variation in scores *within* this country. To do so is roughly analogous to proposing an average pollution statistic for the United States that tells us the cleanliness of "American air." Test scores are largely a function of socioeconomic status. Our wealthier students perform very well when compared to other countries; our poorer students do not. And we have a lot more poor children than do other industrialized nations. One example, supplied by Linda Darling-Hammond: "In 2009 U.S. schools with fewer than 10 percent of students in poverty ranked first among all nations on PISA tests in reading, while those serving more than 75 percent of students in poverty scored alongside nations like Serbia, ranking about fiftieth."[7]

5. Why treat learning as if it were a competitive sport? All of these results emphasize rankings more than ratings, which means the question of educational success has been framed in terms of who's beating whom.

a. Education ≠ economy. If our reason for emphasizing students' relative standing (rather than their absolute achievement) has to do with "competitiveness in the twenty-first-century global economy"—a phrase that issues from politicians, businesspeople, and journalists with all the thoughtfulness of a sneeze, then we would do well to ask two questions. The first, based on values, is whether we regard educating children as something that's primarily justified in terms of corporate profits.

The second question, based on facts, is whether the state of a nation's economy is meaningfully affected by the test scores of students in that nation. Various strands of evidence have converged to suggest that the answer is no. For individual students, school achievement is only weakly related to subsequent workplace performance. And for nations, there's little correlation between average test scores and economic vigor, even if you try to connect scores during one period with the economy some years later (when that cohort of students has grown up).

The late Gerald Bracey, for example, found thirty-eight countries whose economies had been rated on the Current Competitiveness Index calculated by the World Economic Forum and whose students' test scores had also been assessed. There was virtually no correlation between countries' scores on the two lists. And it doesn't help to stagger the two so as to compare today's students in a given country with tomorrow's economy (giving the students time to take their place in the workforce). Consider Japan's outstanding test scores in the 1980s and its dismal economic performance in the 1990s.[8] Moreover, Yong Zhao has shown that "PISA scores in reading, math, and sciences are *negatively* correlated with entrepreneurship indicators in almost every category at statistically significant levels."[9]

b. Why is the relative relevant? Once we've debunked the myth that test scores drive economic success, what reason would we have to fret about our country's standing as measured by those scores? What sense does it make to focus on *relative* performance? After all, to say that our students are first or tenth on a list doesn't tell us whether they're doing well or poorly; it gives us no useful information about how much they know or how good our schools are. If all the countries did reasonably well in absolute terms, there would be no shame in being at the bottom. (Nor would "average" be synonymous with "mediocre.") If all the countries did poorly, there would be no glory in being at the top. Exclamatory headlines about how "our" schools are doing compared to "theirs" suggest that we're less concerned with the quality of education than with whether we can chant, "We're Number One!"

c. Hoping foreign kids won't learn? To treat schooling as if it were a competitive sport is not only irrational but morally offensive. If our goal is for

American kids to triumph over those who live elsewhere — to have a better ranking — then the implication is that we want children who live in other countries to fail, at least in relative terms. We want them not to learn successfully just because they're not Americans. That's built into the notion of "competitiveness" (as opposed to excellence or success), which by definition means that one individual or group can succeed only if others don't. This is a troubling way to look at any endeavor, but where children are concerned, it's indefensible. And it's worth pointing out these implications to anyone who uncritically cites the results of an international ranking.

Moreover, rather than defending policies designed to help our graduates "compete," I'd argue that we should make decisions on the basis of what will help them to develop the skills and disposition to *collaborate* effectively. Educators, too, ought to think in terms of working with — and learning from — their counterparts in other countries so that children everywhere will become more proficient and enthusiastic learners. But every time we rank "our" kids against "theirs," that becomes a little less likely to happen.

NOTES

1. Pew Research Center for People and the Press, "Public's Knowledge of Science and Technology," April 22, 2013. Available at www.people-press.org/2013/04/22/publics-knowledge-of-science-and-technology/.

2. W. Wayt Gibbs and Douglas Fox, "The False Crisis in Science Education," *Scientific American*, October 1999: 87–92.

3. Erling E. Boe and Sujie Shin, "Is the United States Really Losing the International Horse Race in Academic Achievement?" *Phi Delta Kappan*, May 2005: 688–95.

4. National Center for Economic Statistics, *Average Performance of U.S. Students Relative to International Peers on the Most Recent International Assessments in Reading, Mathematics, and Science: Results from PIRLS 2006, TIMSS 2007, and PISA 2009*, 2011. Available at http://nces.ed.gov/surveys/international/reports/2011-mrs.asp.

5. See, for example, Alfie Kohn, *The Case Against Standardized Testing* (Heinemann, 2000); or Phillip Harris et al., *The Myths of Standardized Tests* (Rowman & Littlefield, 2011).

6. For example, see Iris C. Rotberg, "Interpretation of International Test Score Comparisons," *Science*, May 15, 1998: 1030–31.

7. Linda Darling-Hammond, "Redlining Our Schools," *The Nation*, January 30, 2012: 12. Also see Mel Riddile, "PISA: It's Poverty Not Stupid," *The Principal Difference* [NASSP blog], December 15, 2010; and Martin Carnoy and Richard Rothstein, "What Do International Tests Really Show About U.S. Student Performance?" Economic Policy Institute report, January 28, 2013. Available at www.epi.org/publication/us-student-performance-testing/.

8. Keith Baker, "High Test Scores: The Wrong Road to National Economic Success," *Kappa Delta Pi Record*, Spring 2011: 116–20; Zalman Usiskin, "Do We Need National Standards with Teeth?" *Educational Leadership*, November 2007: 40; and Gerald W. Bracey, "Test Scores and Economic Growth," *Phi Delta Kappan*, March 2007: 554–56. "The reason is clear," says Iris Rotberg. "Other variables, such as outsourcing to gain access to lower-wage employees, the climate and incentives for innovation, tax rates, health-care and retirement costs, the extent of government subsidies or partnerships, protectionism, intellectual-property enforcement, natural resources, and exchange rates overwhelm mathematics and science scores in predicting economic competitiveness" ("International Test Scores, Irrelevant Policies," *Education Week*, September 14, 2001: 32).

9. Yong Zhao, "Flunking Innovation and Creativity," *Phi Delta Kappan*, September 2012: 58. Emphasis added.

CHAPTER 2

Competitiveness vs. Excellence

"What's the matter with us?" demands Bob Herbert in his August 7, 2010 *New York Times* column. "The latest dismal news on the leadership front" proving that we've become "a nation of nitwits" comes courtesy of a report from the College Board, he says. "At a time when a college education is needed more than ever to establish and maintain a middle-class standard of living, America's young people are moving in exactly the wrong direction."

"The educational capacity of our country continues to decline," Herbert quotes the report as saying, adding that this is "beyond pathetic."

Now, one could take issue with this alarmist rhetoric on the grounds that our well-being (as individuals and as a society) is once again being framed in purely economic terms: The benefits of education are measured by the size of one's future paychecks. Or one could point out that, even from an economic perspective, we're blaming the victims here. There aren't nearly enough high-paying jobs even for those with impressive credentials, and projections suggest that the vast majority of jobs expected to be created in the years ahead will not require a college degree.

But there's a more basic problem with Herbert's column—and with a similarly themed speech that President Obama delivered at the University of Texas. Its premise is dead wrong. If we want more people to attend and graduate from college than currently do so, the trend has actually been in exactly the right direction for quite some time.

In the College Board report that Herbert cited, you will find a graph showing that the percentage of twenty-five- to thirty-four-year-olds with an

---

"Competitiveness vs. Excellence" was originally published as a blog post on August 9, 2010.

associate degree or higher was 38 percent in 2000 and has edged up pretty steadily since then. As of the last year shown, 2008, it had reached 42 percent.

For the bigger picture, we need to go back farther. The most readily available figures use a slightly different metric: the proportion of adults at least twenty-five years old who have completed four or more years of college. In 1970, only 11 percent had done so. In 1980, it was up to 17 percent. In 1990, 21 percent. In 2000, 26 percent. In 2009, 30 percent.

Now we may say, "That's still not high enough." But how in the world do these numbers support the conclusion that we're moving in "exactly the wrong direction"? The operative phrase in that question, it turns out, is "in the world." Herbert (like the College Board and the president) doesn't seem to be interested in whether we're making progress. The only question of interest is whether the U.S. is beating other countries.

It turns out that people of other nationalities have the audacity to want their students, too, to get more education. And they, too, are making progress toward that goal. Like most op-ed columnists, reporters, and politicians (of both parties), Herbert actually regards this fact as bad news.

From any reasonable moral standard, we'd want kids to succeed regardless of where they call home. If progress were being made worldwide, that would be terrific news. But what kind of standard is it when the goal isn't success (for all) but merely victory (for America)? Even if we're talking only about economics, it's worth rethinking our zero-sum assumption. In an article in *Foreign Affairs* called "Competitiveness: A Dangerous Obsession," Paul Krugman showed why it's simply inaccurate to believe that other countries have to fail in order for our country to succeed.[1] (The late economist David M. Gordon made essentially the same point in *The Atlantic*; his essay was titled "Do We Need to Be No. 1?")

And when we're talking about education — how effectively students are learning, or how long they remain in school — the preoccupation with rankings is even less appropriate, as I argued in chapter 1.

The toxicity of a competitive worldview is such that even people who are reasonably progressive on other issues literally don't notice evidence that's staring them in the face — in this case, showing that more and more of our population are getting college degrees with each passing year. When we're perpetually worried about being — and staying — king of the mountain, we find ourselves taking a position that leads us to view progress made by young people in other countries as bad news.

Maybe Bob Herbert is right after all to ask "What's the matter with us?"

NOTE

1. Paul Krugman, "Competitiveness: A Dangerous Obsession," *Foreign Affairs*, March–April 1994. Available at http://bit.ly/ciywlL.

CHAPTER 3

What Passes for School Reform
"Value-Added" Teacher Evaluation and Other Absurdities

The less people know about teaching and learning, the more sympathetic they're likely to be to the kind of "school reform" that's all the rage these days. Look, they say, some teachers (and schools) are lousy, aren't they? And we want kids to receive a better education—including poor kids, who typically get the short end of the stick, right? So let's rock the boat a little! Clean out the dead wood, close down the places that don't work, slap public ratings on these suckers just like restaurants that have to display the results of their health inspections.

On my sunnier days, I manage to look past the ugliness of the media's relentless disparagement of teachers and the fact that the editorials and columns about education in every major newspaper and newsweekly in the U.S. seem to have been written by the same person, all reflecting an uncritical acceptance of the Bush-Obama-Gates version of school reform. I try to put it all down to mere ignorance and tamp down darker suspicions about what's going on. If I squeeze my eyes tightly, I can almost see how a reasonable person, someone who doesn't want to widen the *real* gap between the haves and have-nots (which is what tends to happen when attention is focused on the gap in test scores), might look at what's going on and think that it sounds like common sense.

"What Passes for School Reform: 'Value-Added' Teacher Evaluation and Other Absurdities" was originally published as a blog post on September 9, 2010.

Unfortunately, the people who know the most about the subject tend to work in the field of education, which means their protests can be dismissed. Educational theorists and researchers are just "educationists" with axes to grind, hopelessly out of touch with real classrooms. And the people who spend their days *in* real classrooms, teaching our children — well, they're just afraid of being held accountable, aren't they? (Actually, proponents of corporate-style school reform find it tricky to attack teachers, per se, so they train their fire instead on the unions that represent them.) Once the people who do the educating have been excluded from a conversation about how to fix education, we end up hearing mostly from politicians, corporate executives, and journalists.

This type of reform consists of several interlocking parts, powered by a determination to "test kids until they beg for mercy," as the late Ted Sizer once put it. Test scores are accepted on faith as a proxy for quality, which means we can evaluate teachers on the basis of how much value they've added — "value" meaning nothing more than higher scores. That, in turn, paves the way for manipulation by rewards and punishments: Dangle more money in front of the good teachers (with some kind of pay-for-performance scheme), and shame or fire the bad ones. Kids, too, can be paid for jumping through hoops. (It's not a coincidence that this incentive-driven model is favored by economists, who have a growing influence on educational matters and who still tend to accept a behaviorist paradigm that most of psychology left behind ages ago.)

"Reform" also means diverting scarce public funds to charter schools, many of them run by for-profit corporations. It means standardizing what's taught (and ultimately tested) from coast to coast, as if uniformity was synonymous with quality. It means reducing job security for teachers, even though tenure just provides due-process protections so people can't be sacked arbitrarily. It means attacking unions at every opportunity, thereby winning plaudits from the folks who, no matter what the question, mutter menacingly about how the damned unions are to blame.

And of course it means describing as "a courageous challenge to the failed status quo" what is really just an intensification of the same tactics that have been squeezing the life out of our classrooms for a good quarter-century now. That intensification has been a project of the Obama administration, even though, as Rep. John Kline (R-MN) remarked, in its particulars it comes "straight from the traditional Republican playbook."

We can show that merit pay is counterproductive, that closing down struggling schools (or firing principals) makes no sense, that charters have a spotty record overall, that high-stakes testing has never been shown to produce any benefit other than higher scores on other standardized tests (and even that only sporadically). To make these points is not to deny that there are some lousy teachers out there. Of course there are. But there are far more good teachers who are being turned *into* bad teachers as a direct result of these policies.

How do such strategies get to be called "school reform" — as opposed to "one particular, highly debatable version of school reform"? Partly, as I say, because those in the best position to challenge them have been preemptively silenced, but also because the so-called reformers are expert at framing the issue. They know that if the focal question is "Don't you agree that a lot of schools stink?" or "Shouldn't we hold teachers and schools accountable?" then they have the advantage. They can present their slash-and-burn tactics as "better than nothing" (as if nothing were the only alternative) or as "tough medicine" (even though what they're peddling is worse than the disease it's supposed to cure).

What if we asked other questions instead? We could do so about any of the policies I've mentioned, but for now let's consider the idea of judging teachers with a "value-added" method.

Question 1: Does this model provide valid and reliable information about teachers (and schools)? Most experts in the field of educational assessment say, "Good heavens, no." This year's sterling teacher may well look like crud next year, and vice versa. Too many variables affect a cohort's test scores; statistically speaking, we just can't credit or blame any individual teacher.

Unfortunately, many of the experts who point this out tend to stop there, even though the problem runs far deeper than technical psychometric flaws with the technique. For example . . .

Question 2: Does learning really lend itself to *any* kind of "value-added" approach? It does only if it's conceived as an assembly line process in which children are filled up with facts and skills at each station along a conveyor belt, and we need only insert a dipstick before and after they arrive at a given station (say, fourth grade), measure the pre/post difference, and judge the worker at that station accordingly. The very idea of "value-added measures," not just a specific formula for calculating them, implicitly accepts this absurd model.

Question 3: Do standardized tests assess what matters most about teaching and learning? If not, then no value-added approach based on those tests makes any sense. As I've argued elsewhere — and of course I'm hardly alone in doing so — test results primarily tell us two things: the socioeconomic status of the students being tested and the amount of time devoted to preparing students for a particular test.

Regarding individual students, at least three studies have found a statistically significant positive relationship between high scores on standardized tests and a relatively shallow approach to learning. Regarding individual teachers, let's just say that some of the best the field has to offer do not necessarily raise their kids' test scores (because they're too busy helping the kids to become enthusiastic and proficient thinkers, which is not what the tests measure), while some teachers who *are* very successful at raising test scores are not much good at anything else. Finally, regarding whole schools, if test scores rise enough, and for long enough, to suggest a trend rather than a fluke, the rational response from a local parent would be, "Uh-oh. What was sacrificed from our children's education in order to make *that* happen?"

It won't do to fall back on the tired slogan that test scores may not be perfect, but they're good enough. The more you examine the construction of these exams, the more likely you are to conclude that they do not add any useful information to what can be learned from other, more authentic forms of assessment. In fact, they actively detract from our understanding about learning (and teaching) because their results are so misleading.

Notice, by the way, that everyone who declares that we ought to reward good teachers and boot the bad ones is assuming that all of us agree on what *good* and *bad* mean. But do we? I'd argue that a dipstick, test-based model is endorsed by newspapers, by public officials, and by billionaires who have bought their seat at the policy-making table (seat, hell; they own the table itself) precisely because we often *don't* agree.

Imagine a teacher who gives students plenty of worksheets to complete in class as well as a substantial amount of homework, who emphasizes the connection between studying hard and getting good grades, who is clearly in control of the class, insisting that students raise their hands and wait patiently to be recognized, who prepares detailed lesson plans well ahead of time, uses the latest textbooks, gives regular quizzes to make sure kids stay on track, and imposes consequences to enforce rules that have been laid out clearly from the beginning. Plenty of parents would move mountains to get their children into that teacher's classroom. I'd do whatever I could to get my children *out*.

Of course people disagree about good education, just as they may not see eye to eye about which movies or restaurants are good. We may never change each other's minds, but we ought to have the chance to try, to discuss our criteria and reflect on how we arrived at them. As Deborah Meier likes to point out, disagreement is both valuable and inevitable in a democratic society. *Un*democratic societies attempt to conceal the disagreement, imposing a single, simple standard from above—and, worse, use that standard to make decisions that can ruin people's lives: which teachers will be humiliated or even fired, which kids will be denied a diploma or forced to repeat a grade, which schools will be shut down. A productive discussion about who's a good teacher (and why) is less likely to take place when the people with the power get to enforce what becomes the definition of quality by default: high scores on bad tests.

I don't expect the founder of a computer empire like Bill Gates or a newspaper editor to understand the art of helping children to understand ideas or of constructing tasks to assess that process. I just expect them to have the humility, the simple decency, not to impose their ignorance on the rest of us with the force of law.

To fight back, an awful lot of teachers who have been celebrated for their students' high scores—those teachers who can't be accused of sour grapes—will have to stand up and say, "Thanks, but let's be honest. All of us who work in schools know that you can't tell how good a teacher is on the basis of his or her kids' test results. In fact, by being forced to think about those results, my colleagues and I are held back from being as good as we can be. By singling me out for commendation—and holding other teachers up to ridicule—you've lowered the quality of schooling for all kids."

CHAPTER 4

STEM Sell
Do Math and Science Matter More Than Other Subjects?

What's the single most alarming educational crisis today? That's easy. It's our failure to pay more attention to the academic field of whichever educator happens to be speaking at the moment.

Just listen, then, and learn that while there may be other problems, too, the truly urgent issue these days is that we're just not investing in math and science instruction the way we should be — with predictably dismaying results. No, it's that kids are outrageously ignorant about history, a subject that ought to be, but never is, a priority. No, it's that even in high school, students still can't write a coherent paragraph. No, the *real* emergency is that reading skills are far from what they should be. No, it's that music and the arts are shamefully neglected in our schools. And so on.

Now, there may be some truth to all of these assertions, and the overarching tragedy is our failure to commit to — and adequately fund — education itself. How unsettling, then, to be overwhelmed by a cacophony of claims by educators from different departments forced to compete for attention.

(Let it also be noted that, if we look carefully, not all of these statements are actually comparable: Saying that a specific subject is underfunded or ignored is different from saying that students are doing poorly in that subject, and vice versa. And saying that either of those things is true with respect to

"STEM Sell: Do Math and Science Matter More Than Other Subjects?" was originally published as a blog post on February 16, 2011.

an ideal standard is different from saying that it's true relative to what happens in other subjects.)

What interests me at the moment, though, are not empirical claims about who's getting what — or the competence that students do or don't possess in a given discipline — but value-based beliefs about what matters most. Does one subject merit special attention, deserve more dollars, constitute the core of what we expect our schools to offer?

To listen to those who shape our society's conversation about education — not educators but public officials, corporate executives, and journalists — the answer is yes. At the top of the heap sits the compound discipline of science, technology, engineering, and math (STEM). Thus, for example, in late 2010 President Obama announced an expensive new public-private initiative called "Educate to Innovate" that will focus on improving student performance exclusively in STEM subjects. A couple of months later, he was back with a new education project. Was its intent to spread the wealth to other kinds of learning that he had overlooked before? Nope. It was to commit another quarter-billion dollars to improve the teaching of STEM subjects. And a few weeks later, in his State of the Union address, the only academic disciplines he mentioned were, yet again, math and science.

Thought experiment: Try to imagine this, or any other, president giving a speech that calls for a major new commitment to the teaching of literature, backed by generous funding (even during a period of draconian budget cuts). Close your eyes and hear our chief executive's stirring words:

> Few experiences can compare to savoring truly wonderful fiction, and our obligation is to make sure that all children are invited to do just that. Moreover, we must help them to appreciate what they're reading and encourage them to continue reading for pleasure throughout their lives. At its best, literature enriches our understanding of the human condition and the natural world, while thrilling us with words arranged in combinations that are unexpected and yet perfectly right. The appreciation of the literary imagination is a hallmark of a truly civilized society, yet we have fallen woefully short of making this a priority in our schools. That is why I am announcing today a commitment of $3 billion to establish . . .

Yeah. Right.

The point of my example is not to argue in favor of studying literature, per se, or, for that matter, to argue against studying math and science. It is to ask a question rarely posed except by educators in other fields — namely, why STEM subjects consistently attract so much money and attention.

Among decision leaders and the general public, I suspect that STEM enjoys an immediate advantage simply because it tends to involve numbers. Our society is inclined to regard any topic as more compelling if it can be expressed in numerical terms. Notice how rarely we evaluate schools by their impact on students' *interest* in learning; we focus on precisely specified achievement effects. Issues that inherently seem qualitative in nature — intrinsic motivation, say, or the meaning of life — we consign to the ivory tower. And when questions that don't lend themselves to quantification aren't simply brushed aside, they're reduced to numbers anyway. Witness, for example, how English teachers have been told that they not only can but must use rubrics to quantify their responses to students' writings.

As compared with other, "softer" disciplines, STEM usually provides us with the reassurance of knowing exactly how much, how many, how far, how fast, which means that these subjects are viewed (often incorrectly) as being inherently objective, therefore more reliable (another questionable leap), and therefore more valuable (yet another one).[1]

Closely related to our comfort with numbers, then, is our preference for practicality. But STEM seems practical with respect to a specific kind of number — namely, dollars. Putting aside for the moment the fact that reading and writing skills, too, have obvious implications for real-world success — and, conversely, that theoretical physics and "pure" mathematics do not — it's easy to see how politicians and corporate leaders would favor the fields that appear to be more directly linked to economic productivity and profit.

Moreover, anyone whose sensibility is shaped by a zero-sum mindset, such that the goal is not success but victory, is far more likely to be drawn to STEM subjects than to the humanities. "The nation that out-educates us today," said President Obama, "is going to out-compete us tomorrow." That is a sentence that could have been spoken by the most reactionary Republican you can name. But it is not a sentence likely to be followed by a discussion of the humanities. Those who confuse excellence with competitiveness are most likely to privilege STEM subjects over others — and vice versa.

Every educator — in fact, every citizen — needs to know how profoundly mistaken are the specific empirical claims that we keep hearing on C-SPAN regarding the relationship between school achievement and jobs, and regarding the relative status of U.S. students. Yong Zhao recently did a fine job of rebutting the specific contentions enunciated in the State of the Union address.[2] As Harold Salzman and B. Lindsay Lowell have reported, very few jobs require advanced proficiency in STEM subjects, and there is actually "an ample supply of [science and engineering] students whose preparation and performance has been increasing over the past decades." In fact, "each year there are more than three times as many [science and engineering] four-year college graduates as S&E job openings."[3]

But my point here is more basic. The real question we should be asking when we hear yet another speech arguing, explicitly or implicitly, for the unique importance of STEM disciplines is What does this say about the speaker's—or our society's—beliefs about the point of education itself? You don't have to be a music or history teacher to say, "Now, hold on a minute!" In fact, even algebra teachers should be frowning because the reasons for a politician's (or the Chamber of Commerce's) STEM-centricity carry implications for what's taught *within* a STEM course, and *how* it's taught, and whether K–12 education is conceived as nothing more than an elaborate, extended exercise in vocational preparation.

Building on a discussion by the educational historian David Labaree, I once created a simple table, which you can see on the following page, to capture four possible purposes for schooling our children. I am troubled by both the private and public versions of an economic focus, and I am drawn to what, for lack of a better word, might be called the humanistic purposes— again, in both their private and public expressions.

Yet another respected thinker who recoiled from the educational priorities reflected in President Obama's State of the Union message was Berkeley linguist Robin Lakoff, who called on us to recognize education's "less practical (but equally vital) functions." [4] She added that "education is invaluable not only in its ability to help people and societies get ahead, but equally in helping them develop the perspectives that make them fully human."

Anyone who agrees with that sentiment—and who worries at least as much about the state of our democracy as about the state of the Dow Jones Industrial Average—should think not only about education in general but about which subjects are seen as priorities within the field of education. And why.

POSSIBLE PURPOSES OF SCHOOLS		
	private	public
humanistic	to enhance personal fulfillment	to build a democratic society
economic	to maximize one's own competitive financial success	to increase corporate profits

From Alfie Kohn, *The Schools Our Children Deserve* (Houghton Mifflin, 1999). Copyright © 1999 by Alfie Kohn.

NOTES

1. For more on this topic, see chapter 9 ("Schooling Beyond Measure").

2. See Yong Zhao, "'It Makes No Sense': Puzzling over Obama's State of the Union Speech," blog post, January 30, 2011. Available at http://ow.ly/DEfNl.

3. See B. Lindsay Lowell and Hal Salzman, "Into the Eye of the Storm: Assessing the Evidence on Science and Engineering Education, Quality, and Workforce Demand," October 2007. Available at http://policy.rutgers.edu/faculty/salzman/411562_Salzman_Science.pdf.

4. See Robin Lakoff, "Education: Yes, but Why?" *Huffington Post*, February 2, 2011. Available at http://ow.ly/HoNOf.

CHAPTER 5

How to Sell Conservatism
Lesson 1—Pretend You're a Reformer

If you somehow neglected to renew your subscription to the *Journal of Personality and Social Psychology*, you may have missed a couple of interesting articles. A series of studies conducted by two independent groups of researchers (published in the September and November 2009 issues, respectively) added to an already substantial collection of evidence showing that "people are motivated to perceive existing social arrangements as just and legitimate."[1]

As is common with social psych studies, all the subjects were college students, so extrapolate to every other member of our species at your peril. Still, in a variety of different experiments, everything from the formula used by a university for funding its departments to unequal gender arrangements in business or politics was likely to be regarded as fair simply because, well, that's how things are already being done. Subjects also tended to prefer the taste of a beverage if they were told it was an established brand than if they were told it was new.

If possession is nine-tenths of the law, then existence apparently is nine-tenths of rightness. At the same time, though, we seem to enjoy the smell of fresh paint (as Sartre put it). There's something undeniably alluring about the new-and-improved version of whatever product we're used to buying—as long as the product itself hasn't changed too much. We may be seized by an urge to throw the bums out every other November, but don't ask

"How to Sell Conservatism: Lesson 1—Pretend You're a Reformer" was originally published as a blog post on October 20, 2010.

us to question the two-party system itself. After all, if that's how things are done, it must be for good reason.

For a shrewd policy maker, then, the ideal formula would seem to be to let people enjoy the invigorating experience of demanding reform without having to give up whatever they're used to. And that's precisely what both liberals and conservatives manage to do: Advertise as a daring departure from the status quo what is actually just a slightly new twist on it.

But conservatives have gone a step further. They've figured out how to take policies that actually represent an *intensification* of the status quo and dress them up as something that's long overdue. In many cases the values and practices they endorse have already been accepted, but they try to convince us they've lost so they can win even more.

This phenomenon is easiest to notice in the realm of public policy. It's pretty obvious to all but the most doctrinaire libertarian that the financial cataclysm of 2007–2008, from which we've yet to recover, was a direct result of inadequate regulation of the investment banking industry. (Even Ayn Rand protégé Alan Greenspan admitted that his faith in the free market was, er, somewhat misplaced.) This failure to regulate, in turn, reflects a sneering distrust of government that has been carefully cultivated at least since Ronald Reagan took office thirty years ago. And of course it's not limited to banking. The private sector's license to function with minimal oversight seems to have played a leading role in one recent disaster after another, from the catastrophic BP oil spill to mine and gas line explosions to food recalls.

Yet those who have drunk the ideological Kool-Aid—a lot more than tea is served at these parties—portray themselves as revolutionaries by virtue of demanding even further restrictions on the ability of democratically elected officials to regulate corporate conduct in the public interest. By framing the primary threat to our well-being as Big Government, conservatives succeed in marketing as something qualitatively new and different what is actually a ramped-up version of the very free-market dogma whose consequences we've been experiencing for quite some time.

Interestingly, this same artful maneuver also shows up far from the domain of Goldman Sachs and BP. Consider the way children are raised in our culture. I think it can be argued that the dominant problem with parenting isn't permissiveness; it's a *fear* of permissiveness that leads us to be excessively controlling. For every example of a child who is permitted to run wild in a public place, there are hundreds of examples of children being restricted unnecessarily, yelled at, threatened, or bullied by their parents, children whose protests are routinely ignored and whose questions are dismissed out of hand, children who have become accustomed to hearing an automatic "No!" in response to their requests, and a "Because I said so!" if they ask for a reason.

But traditionalists—who, when it comes to children, include a discouraging number of political liberals—have persuaded us to ignore the epidemic of punitive parenting and focus instead on the occasional example of overindulgence—sometimes even to the point of pronouncing an entire generation spoiled. (It's revealing that similar alarms have been raised for decades, if not centuries.[2]) To create the impression that kids today are out of control is to justify a call for even tighter restrictions, tougher discipline, more punishment. And, again, this is billed as a courageous departure from contemporary parenting practices rather than identified for what it is: an intensification of the control-oriented model that has already done incalculable damage.

Consider, finally, the case of education. Seymour Papert, known for his work on artificial intelligence, began one of his books by inviting us to imagine a group of surgeons and a group of teachers, both from a century ago, who are magically transported to the present day. The surgeons visit a modern operating room and struggle to understand what's going on, but the teachers feel right at home in today's schools. Kids, they discover, are still segregated by age in rows of classrooms; are still made to sit passively and listen (or practice skills) most of the time; are still tested and graded, rewarded or punished; still set against one another in contests and deprived of any real say about what they're doing.

Those tempted to point defensively to updates in the delivery system only end up underscoring how education is still about delivering knowledge to empty receptacles. In fact, snazzier technology—say, posting grades or homework assignments on-line—mostly serves to distract us from rethinking the pedagogy. Interactive whiteboards in classrooms amount to a twenty-first-century veneer on old-fashioned, teacher-centered instruction.

But enter now the school "reformers": get-tough superintendents; big-money corporate types; Secretary of Education Arne Duncan and his ideological soulmates who preceded him in the Bush administration; and the reporters, editorial writers, and producers at just about every mass media outlet in the U.S. School reform, as these people understand it, and as I discussed in chapter 3, involves a relentless regimen of standardized testing; a push to direct funds to charter schools, many of them run by for-profit corporations; a weakening of teachers' job protection—and the vilification of unions that represent teachers—so that those who have failed to raise their students' test scores can be publicly humiliated or fired; threats to shut down low-scoring schools; initiatives to dangle money in front of teachers who follow orders and raise scores, or even in front of certain (low-income) students; and a contest for funding in which only (some) states willing to adopt this bribe-and-threat agenda will receive desperately needed federal money.

This business-style version of reform is routinely described as "bold" or "daring"—in contrast to the "failed status quo," which is blamed on the teachers' unions. (With education, just as with parenting, even people who are reasonably progressive on other issues suddenly sound as if they're auditioning for Fox News.) There's much to be said about each of the policies I've listed, but for now the point to be emphasized is that, just as with the Tea Party members who rally to stop the "tyranny" of mild federal checks on corporate power, or the parenting writers who urge us to "dare to discipline" our children (even though 94 percent of parents of preschoolers admit to spanking their children), the school reformers are in fact accelerating what has already been happening over the last couple of decades.

Even before the implementation of what should be called the Many Children Left Behind Act, states and school districts were busy standardizing curricula, imposing more and more tests, and using an array of rewards and punishments to pressure teachers and students to fall in line—with the most extreme version of this effort reserved for the inner cities. Before anyone outside of Texas had heard of George W. Bush, many of us had been calling attention to the fact that these policies were turning schools into glorified test-prep centers, driving some of the most innovative teachers to leave the profession, and increasing the drop-out rate among kids of color.

Yet the so-called reformers have succeeded in convincing people that their top-down, test-driven approach—in effect, the status quo on steroids—is a courageous rejection of what we've been doing.

Here's what *would* be new: questioning all the stuff that Papert's early-twentieth-century visitors would immediately recognize: a regimen of memorizing facts and practicing skills that features lectures, worksheets, quizzes, report cards, and homework. But the Gates-Bush-Obama version of "school reform" not only fails to call those things into question; it actually intensifies them, particularly in urban schools. The message, as educator Harvey Daniels observed, consists of saying in effect that "what we're doing [in the classroom] is OK, we just need to do it harder, longer, stronger, louder, meaner."

Real education reform would require us to consider the elimination of many features that we've come to associate with school, so perhaps the reluctance to take such suggestions seriously is just a specific instance of the "whatever is, is right" bias that psychologists keep documenting. At the same time, traditionalists — educational or otherwise — know that it's politically advantageous to position themselves as being outside the establishment. Our challenge is to peer through the fog of rhetoric, to realize that what's being billed as reform should seem distinctly familiar — and not particularly welcome.

NOTES

1. The studies are, respectively, Aaron C. Kay et al., "Inequality, Discrimination, and the Power of the Status Quo," *Journal of Personality and Social Psychology* 97 (2009): 421–34; and S. Eidelman et al., "The Existence Bias," *Journal of Personality and Social Psychology* 97 (2009): 765–75.

2. See Alfie Kohn, *The Myth of the Spoiled Child* (Da Capo, 2014), chapter 1.

CHAPTER 6

Operation Discourage Bright People from Wanting to Teach

Education "reformers" have discovered the source of our schools' problems. It's not poverty or social inequities. It's not enforced student passivity or a standardized curriculum that consists of lists of facts and skills likely to appear on standardized tests. No—it's . . . teachers.

Fortunately, there's a two-pronged solution: First, identify the really bad teachers (on the basis of their students' test scores, naturally), and pluck them out like weeds. Second, as a safeguard against the possibility of more widespread incompetence than can be solved by step #1, remove as much authority as possible—about what's to be taught and how—from *all* teachers.

Two articles in the October 2010 issue of *Phi Delta Kappan* address these strategies. "Incompetent Teachers or Dysfunctional Systems?" by Ken Futernick looks carefully at the premises—and real-world effects—of sacking teachers who fail to perform up to expectations. And Maja Wilson's "'There Are a Lot of Really Bad Teachers Out There'" weighs efforts to improve teaching by imposing mandates from above.

We should begin by noting that claims about the contribution of the quality of teaching to student success are often overstated, particularly by "reformers." As Richard Rothstein reminds us, all school-related variables combined can explain only about one-third of the variation in student achievement; most is due to non-school factors.[1] Still, even to the extent that the quality of teaching does matter, Futernick argues that "variations in

"Operation Discourage Bright People from Wanting to Teach" was originally published as a blog post on November 1, 2010.

teaching performance flow largely from variables that have little to do with the qualities of teachers themselves." Lousy classrooms are more likely due to "poorly functioning systems than [to] individual [teachers'] shortcomings."

If, for example, a lot of *good* teachers are quitting, or are assigned to teach subjects outside their areas of expertise, then a purge of bad teachers isn't going to help—particularly if that district doesn't have better teachers waiting in the wings to replace them. Moreover, the "bad" teachers may not really be bad at all. Futernick points out that they may just "lack adequate support and resources" that would allow them to succeed. Not only is it unfair to blame them for what is really a systemic failure, it doesn't help kids because that failure will persist even after we shuffle the personnel.

Of course it's a lot easier to pretend the problem rests primarily with incompetent individuals and, therefore, that all would be well if we could just eliminate tenure and those damned unions that make it hard to get rid of slackers (or anyone else an administrator would like to fire for whatever reason). In the meantime, though, the Powers That Be are producing uniform standards and curricula that will let them impose their will on classrooms from a distance. "If we can't get rid of teachers' physical selves," says Maja Wilson, "we can replace their teaching selves with the standardized self of the mandated, scripted curriculum" and thereby assure quality.

But whose definition of "quality"? Arne Duncan and Bill Gates have no better grasp of the nuances of how children learn, and what constitutes meaningful evidence of deep understanding, than does your next-door neighbor—which helps to explain why, when they talk about "quality" (or "achievement"), all they mean is higher standardized test scores. Unlike your neighbor, though, they have the power to compel schools—whole states, even—to enact practices that will cement that conflation into place.

Let's assume for the sake of the argument, though, that some people in a position of power really do have an unusually good feel for how children learn. Wilson's point is that great teaching can't be imposed from above: "Mandating practices in the effort to improve teaching paradoxically creates the kind of environment that undermines good teaching . . . by stunt[ing] teachers' ability to make good decisions in the classroom."

There is simply no shortcut to helping educators "cultivate an active intelligence that allows them to negotiate principles, practices, students' needs, and the ever-changing classroom and school environment," says Wilson. In short, she adds (in a sentence that ought to be e-mailed to every administrator and consultant in the country), "Good teaching doesn't rest on specific practices, but on how well the educator actively thinks through hundreds of decisions that no program can script." To *try* to mandate specific practices — and Wilson offers some disconcerting examples relating to "literacy systems" — not only doesn't help teachers to become more accomplished, flexible thinkers; it gets in the way.

Efforts to fire bad teachers and mandate specific practices weren't devised in a vacuum. They emerge from a specific cultural context. Specifically, this double-barreled strategy seems to reflect:

- an arrogance on the part of decision makers that expresses itself in a predilection for top-down control — doing things *to* people rather than working *with* them

- the low esteem in which the profession of teaching is held (It would seem outrageous for professionals in most other fields to be told how to do their jobs, particularly by people who aren't even in their field.)

- a widespread tendency to blame individuals rather than examining the structural causes of problems — something that distorts our understanding of such varied topics as cheating, self-discipline, competition, character education, and classroom management

- the outsize influence on education of business-oriented models, with a particular emphasis on quantification and standardization, and

- the assumption that teaching consists of filling up little pails with information. If learning were understood instead as the active construction of ideas, it would seem odd, to say the least, to mandate certain teaching styles or a single curriculum for all students at a given grade level.

While there's no official name for the dual strategy of micromanaging teachers and trying to root out the bad ones, it might as well be called Operation Discourage Bright People from Wanting to Teach. After all, who would choose to focus on test preparation rather than helping kids to think and question? Who would agree to forego any real professional autonomy? Who would want to be treated like a pet, rewarded with financial doggie biscuits for toeing the line? And who, if he or she had other opportunities, would pick a career that featured a constant threat of public humiliation?

In fact, it does seem likely that more and more college students who become teachers will be those who *lack* other opportunities. The impact of this isn't difficult to predict. What's less obvious is the ironic fact that it's due, in large part, to what's known — and uncritically celebrated in the popular press — as "school reform."

NOTE

1. See Richard Rothstein, *How to Fix Our Schools*, Economic Policy Institute report (October 4, 2010). Available at epi.org/publication/ib286.

CHAPTER 7

Remember When We Had High Standards? Neither Do I

"In recent years, parents have cried in dismay that their children could not read out loud, could not spell, could not write clearly," while "employers have said that mechanics could not read simple directions. Many a college has blamed high schools for passing on students . . . who could not read adequately to study college subjects; high schools have had to give remedial reading instruction to boys and girls who did not learn to read properly in elementary schools."

On and on goes the devastating indictment of our education system. Or—well, perhaps I shouldn't say "our" education system, since few of us had much to say about school policy when this article appeared . . . in 1954.[1]

Similar jeremiads were published, of course, in the 1980s (see especially the Reagan administration's influential and deeply dishonest "Nation at Risk" report)[2] and in the 1970s, but one could argue that those, like today's denunciations of falling standards and demands for accountability, reflect the same legacy of multiculturalism, radical education professors, and the post-Woodstock cultural realignment that brought down traditional values inside and outside of schools.

But how does one defend such an argument when it turns out that people were saying exactly the same things about America's dysfunctional edu-

---

"Remember When We Had High Standards? Neither Do I" was originally published as a blog post on December 10, 2010.

cation system before Vietnam, before Civil Rights, before feminism—and displaying that same aggressive nostalgia for an earlier era when, you know, excellence really mattered?

And if pundits were throwing up their hands during the *Eisenhower* era about schools on the decline, about students who could barely read and write, about how we're being beaten by [insert name of other country here], the obvious question is: When exactly *was* that golden period that was distinguished by high standards?

The answer, of course, is that it never existed. "The story of declining school quality across the twentieth century is, for the most part, a fable," says social scientist Richard Rothstein, whose book *The Way We Were?* (The Century Foundation, 1998) cites a series of similar attacks on American education, moving backward one decade at a time. Each generation invokes the good old days, during which, we discover, people had been doing exactly the same thing. (Grade inflation is a case in point: Harvard professors were already grumbling about how As were "given too readily" back in 1894, only a few years after letter grades were introduced to the college.)

Of course, this phenomenon isn't limited to schooling. As I've described in my 2014 book *The Myth of the Spoiled Child* (Da Capo Press), claims that parents are too permissive, that they fail to set limits, and consequently that "kids today" are spoiled and self-centered can be found in articles and books that date back decades, if not centuries.

To dig up strikingly familiar observations or sentiments offered by people long dead isn't just an amusing rhetorical flourish. These echoes deprive us of the myth of uniqueness, and that can be usefully unsettling. Whenever we're apt to sound off about how contemporary education—or any other aspect of modern life—is unprecedented in its capacity to give offense, the knowledge that our grandparents or distant ancestors said much the same thing, give or take a superficial detail, serves to remind us of an observation once offered by Adrienne Rich: "Nostalgia is only amnesia turned around."

NOTES

1. John Hersey, "Why Do Students Bog Down on the First R?" *Life*, May 24, 1954: 136. The author adds, "Nor will reading problems be solved by any single, simple panacea, such as 'going back to phonics'" (p. 137)—a caution just as relevant, and just as frequently ignored, today.

2. For details about the misleading claims and tendentious use of data on which the report is based, see David C. Berliner and Bruce J. Biddle, *The Manufactured Crisis* (Reading, MA: Addison Wesley, 1995); and Gerald Bracey, "April Foolishness: The 20th Anniversary of 'A Nation at Risk,'" *Phi Delta Kappan*, April 2003: 616–21.

PART 2

Grades, Tests,

and "Data"

CHAPTER 8

The Case Against Grades

I remember the first time that a grading rubric was attached to a piece of my writing. . . . Suddenly all the joy was taken away. I was writing for a grade— I was no longer exploring for me. I want to get that back. Will I ever get that back?

—Claire, a student (in Olson, 2006)

By now enough has been written about academic assessment to fill a library, but when you stop to think about it, the whole enterprise really amounts to a straightforward two-step dance. We need to collect information about how students are doing, and then we need to share that information (along with our judgments, perhaps) with the students and their parents. Gather and report—that's pretty much it.

You say the devil is in the details? Maybe so, but I'd argue that too much attention to the particulars of implementation may be distracting us from the bigger picture—or at least from a pair of remarkable conclusions that emerge from the best theory, practice, and research on the subject: *Collecting information doesn't require tests, and sharing that information doesn't require grades.* In fact, students would be a lot better off without either of these relics from a less enlightened age.

Why tests are not a particularly useful way to assess student learning (at least the kind that matters), and what thoughtful educators do instead, are questions I address in a preliminary fashion in chapter 12. Here, our task is

---

"The Case Against Grades" was originally published in Educational Leadership *in November 2011. This is a slightly expanded version of the published article.*

to take a hard look at the second practice, the use of letters or numbers as evaluative summaries of how well students have done, regardless of the method used to arrive at those judgments.

THE EFFECTS OF GRADING

Most of the criticisms of grading you'll hear today were laid out forcefully and eloquently anywhere from four to eight decades ago (Crooks, 1933; De Zouche, 1945; Kirschenbaum, Simon, & Napier, 1971; Linder, 1940; Marshall, 1968), and these early essays make for eye-opening reading. They remind us just how long it's been clear there's something wrong with what we're doing as well as just how little progress we've made in acting on that realization.

In the 1980s and '90s, educational psychologists systematically studied the effects of grades. As I've reported elsewhere (Kohn, 1999a, 1999b, 1999c), when students from elementary school to college who are led to focus on grades are compared with those who aren't, the results support three robust conclusions:

- *Grades tend to diminish students' interest in whatever they're learning.* A "grading orientation" and a "learning orientation" have been shown to be inversely related, and, as far as I can tell, every study that has ever investigated the impact on intrinsic motivation of receiving grades (or instructions that emphasize the importance of getting good grades) has found a negative effect.

- *Grades create a preference for the easiest possible task.* Impress upon students that what they're doing will count toward their grade, and their response will likely be to avoid taking any unnecessary intellectual risks. They'll choose a shorter book, or a project on a familiar topic, in order to minimize the chance of doing poorly — not because they're "unmotivated" but because they're rational. They're responding to adults who, by telling them the goal is to get a good mark, have sent the message that success matters more than learning.

- *Grades tend to reduce the quality of students' thinking.* They may skim books for what they'll "need to know." They're less likely to wonder, say, "How can we be sure that's true?" than to ask "Is this going to be on the test?" In one experiment, students told they'd be graded on how well they learned a social studies lesson had more trouble understanding the main point of the text than did students who were told that no grades would be involved. Even on a measure of rote recall, the graded group remembered fewer facts a week later (Grolnick & Ryan, 1987).

Research on the effects of grading has slowed down in the last couple of decades, but the studies that are still being done reinforce the earlier findings. For example, a grade-oriented environment is associated with increased levels of cheating (Anderman & Murdock, 2007), grades (whether or not accompanied by comments) promote a fear of failure even in high-achieving students (Pulfrey et al., 2011), and the elimination of grades (in favor of a pass/fail system) produces substantial benefits with no apparent disadvantages in medical school (White & Fantone, 2010). More important, no recent research has contradicted the earlier "big three" findings, so those conclusions still stand.

WHY GRADING IS INHERENTLY PROBLEMATIC

A student asked his Zen master how long it would take to reach enlightenment. "Ten years," the master said. But, the student persisted, what if he studied very hard? "Then 20 years," the master responded. Surprised, the student asked how long it would take if he worked very, very hard and became the most dedicated student in the ashram. "In that case, 30 years," the master replied. His explanation: "If you have one eye on how close you are to achieving your goal, that leaves only one eye for your task."

To understand why research finds what it does about grades, we need to shift our focus from educational measurement techniques to broader psychological and pedagogical questions. The latter serve to illuminate a series of misconceived assumptions that underlie the use of grading.

Motivation: While it's true that many students, after a few years of traditional schooling, could be described as motivated by grades, what counts is the nature of their motivation. Extrinsic motivation, which includes a desire to get better grades, is not only different from, but often undermines, intrinsic motivation, a desire to learn for its own sake (Kohn 1999a). Many assessment specialists talk about motivation as though it were a single entity — and their recommended practices just put a finer gloss on a system of rewards and punishments that leads students to chase marks and become less interested in the learning itself. If nourishing their *desire* to learn is a primary goal for us, then grading is problematic by its very nature.

Achievement: Two educational psychologists pointed out that "an overemphasis on assessment can actually undermine the pursuit of excellence" (Maehr & Midgley, 1996, p. 7). That unsettling conclusion—which holds regardless of the quality of the assessment but is particularly applicable to the use of grades—is based on these researchers' own empirical findings as well as those of many others, including Carol Dweck, Carole Ames, Ruth Butler, and John Nicholls (for a review, see Kohn, 1999b, chapter 2). In brief: the more students are led to focus on *how well* they're doing, the less engaged they tend to be with *what* they're doing.

It follows that all assessment must be done carefully and sparingly lest students become so concerned about their achievement (how good they are at doing something—or, worse, how their performance compares to others') that they're no longer thinking about the learning itself. Even a well-meaning teacher may produce a roomful of children who are so busy monitoring their own reading skills that they're no longer excited by the stories they're reading. Assessment consultants worry that grades may not accurately reflect student performance; educational psychologists worry because grades fix students' attention *on* their performance.

Quantification: When people ask me, a bit defensively, if it isn't important to measure how well students are learning (or teachers are teaching), I invite them to rethink their choice of verb. There is certainly value in *assessing* the quality of learning and teaching, but that doesn't mean it's always necessary, or even possible, to *measure* those things—that is, to turn them into numbers. Indeed, "measurable outcomes may be the least significant results of learning" (McNeil, 1986, p. xviii)—a realization that offers a refreshing counterpoint to today's corporate-style "school reform" and its preoccupation with data.

To talk about what happens in classrooms, let alone in children's heads, as moving forward or backward in specifiable degrees is not only simplistic, because it fails to capture much of what is going on, but also destructive because it may change what is going on for the worse. Once we're compelled to focus only on what can be reduced to numbers, such as how many grammatical errors are present in a composition or how many mathematical algorithms have been committed to memory, thinking has been severely compromised. And that is exactly what happens when we try to fit learning into a four- or five- or (heaven help us) 100-point scale.

Curriculum: "One can have the best assessment imaginable," Howard Gardner (1991, p. 254) observed, "but unless the accompanying curriculum is of quality, the assessment has no use." Some people in the field are candid about their relativism, offering to help align your assessment to whatever your goals or curriculum may be. The result is that teachers may become more adept at measuring how well students have mastered a collection of facts and skills whose value is questionable—and never questioned. "If it's not worth teaching, it's not worth teaching well," as Eliot Eisner (2001, p. 370) likes to say. Nor, we might add, is it worth assessing accurately.

Portfolios, for example, can be constructive if they replace grades rather than being used to *yield* them. They offer a way to thoughtfully gather a variety of meaningful examples of learning for the students to review. But what's the point "if instruction is dominated by worksheets so that every portfolio looks the same"? (Neill et al., 1995, p. 4). Conversely, one sometimes finds a mismatch between more thoughtful forms of pedagogy—say, a workshop approach to teaching writing—and a depressingly standardized assessment tool like rubrics (Wilson, 2006).

IMPROVING GRADING: A FOOL'S ERRAND?

I had been advocating standards-based grading, which is a very important movement in its own right, but it took a push from some great educators to make me realize that if I wanted to focus my assessment around authentic feedback, then I should just abandon grades altogether.

—New Jersey middle school teacher Jason Bedell (2010)

Much of what is prescribed in the name of "assessing for learning" (and, for that matter, "formative assessment") leaves me uneasy: The recommended practices often seem prefabricated and mechanistic; the imperatives of data collection seem to upstage the children themselves, and the goal of helping them become more enthusiastic about what they're doing. Still, if it's done only occasionally and with humility, I think it's possible to assess for learning. But *grading* for learning is, to paraphrase a 1960's-era slogan, rather like bombing for peace. Rating and ranking students (and their efforts to figure things out) is inherently counterproductive.

If I'm right—more to the point, if all the research to which I've referred is taken seriously—then the absence of grades is a necessary, though not sufficient, condition for promoting deep thinking and a desire to engage in it. It's worth lingering on this proposition in light of a variety of efforts to sell us formulas to improve our grading techniques, none of which address the problems of grading, per se.

• It's not enough to replace letters or numbers with labels ("exceeds expectations," "meets expectations," and so on). If you're sorting students into four or five piles, you're still grading them. Rubrics typically include numbers as well as labels, which is only one of several reasons they merit our skepticism (Wilson, 2006; Kohn, 2006).

• It's not enough to tell students in advance exactly what's expected of them. "When school is seen as a test, rather than an adventure in ideas," teachers may persuade themselves they're being fair "if they specify, in listlike fashion, exactly what must be learned to gain a satisfactory grade . . . [but] such schooling is unfair in the wider sense that it prepares students to pass other people's tests without strengthening their capacity to set their own assignments in collaboration with their fellows" (Nicholls & Hazzard, 1993, p. 77).

• It's not enough to disseminate grades more efficiently—for example, by posting them on-line. There is a growing technology, as the late Gerald Bracey once remarked, "that permits us to do in nanoseconds things that we should-n't be doing at all" (quoted in Mathews, 2006). In fact, posting grades on-line is a significant step backward because it enhances the salience of those grades and therefore their destructive effects on learning.

• It's not enough to add narrative reports. "When comments and grades co-exist, the comments are written to justify the grade" (Wilson, 2009, p. 60). Teachers report that students, for their part, often just turn to the grade and ignore the comment, but "when there's only a comment, they read it," says high school English teacher Jim Drier. Moreover, research suggests that the harmful impact of grades on creativity is no less (and possibly even more) potent when a narrative accompanies them. Narratives are helpful only in the absence of grades (Butler, 1988; Pulfrey et al., 2011).

• It's not enough to use "standards-based" grading. That phrase may suggest any number of things—for example, more consistency, or a reliance on more elaborate formulas, in determining grades; greater specificity about what each grade signifies; or an increase in the number of tasks or skills that are graded. At best, these prescriptions do nothing to address the fundamental problems with grading. At worst, they exacerbate those problems. In addition to the simplistic premise that it's always good to have more data, we find a penchant shared by the behaviorists of yesteryear that learning can and should be broken down into its components, each to be evaluated separately. And more frequent temperature-taking produces exactly the kind of disproportionate attention to performance (at the expense of learning) that researchers have found to be so counterproductive.

The term "standards-based" is sometimes intended just to mean that grading is aligned with a given set of objectives, in which case our first response should be to inquire into the value of those objectives (as well as the extent to which students were invited to help formulate them). If grades are based on state standards, there's particular reason to be concerned since those standards are often too specific, age-inappropriate, superficial, and standardized by definition. In my experience, the best teachers tend to be skeptical about aligning their teaching to a list imposed by distant authorities, or using that list as a basis for assessing how well their students are thinking.

Finally, "standards-based" may refer to something similar to criterion-based testing, where the idea is to avoid grading students on a curve. (Even some teachers who don't do so explicitly nevertheless act as though grades ought to fall into something close to a normal distribution, with only a few students receiving As. But this pattern is not a fact of life, nor is it a sign of admirable "rigor" on the teacher's part. Rather, "it is a symbol of failure—failure to teach well, failure to test well, and failure to have any influence at all on the intellectual lives of students" [Milton, Pollio, & Eison, 1986].) This surely represents an improvement over a system in which the number of top marks is made artificially scarce and students are set against one another. But here we've peeled back the outer skin of the onion (competition) only to reveal more noxious layers beneath: extrinsic motivation, numerical ratings, the tendency to promote achievement at the expense of learning.

If we begin with a desire to assess more often, or to produce more data, or to improve the consistency of our grading, then certain prescriptions will follow. If, however, our point of departure isn't mostly about the grading but about our desire for students to understand ideas from the inside out, or to get a kick out of playing with words and numbers, or to be in charge of their own learning, then we will likely end up elsewhere. We may come to see grading as a huge, noisy, fuel-guzzling, smoke-belching machine that constantly requires repairs and new parts, when what we should be doing is pulling the plug.

DELETING—OR AT LEAST DILUTING—GRADES

"Like it or not, grading is here to stay" is a statement no responsible educator would ever offer as an excuse for inaction. What matters is whether a given practice is in the best interest of students. If it isn't, then our obligation is to work for its elimination and, in the meantime, do what we can to minimize its impact.

Replacing letter and number grades with narrative assessments or conferences—qualitative summaries of student progress offered in writing or as part of a conversation—is not a utopian fantasy. It has already been done successfully in many elementary and middle schools and even in some high schools, both public and private (Kohn, 1999c). It's important not only to realize that such schools exist but to investigate *why* they've eliminated grades, how they've managed to do so (hint: the process can be gradual), and what benefits they have realized.

Naturally objections will be raised to this—or any—significant policy change, but once students and their parents have been shown the relevant research, reassured about their concerns, and invited to participate in constructing alternative forms of assessment, the abolition of grades proves to be not only realistic but an enormous improvement over the status quo. Sometimes it's only after grading has ended that we realize just how harmful it's been.

To address one common fear, the graduates of grade-free high schools are indeed accepted by selective private colleges and large public universities—on the basis of narrative reports and detailed descriptions of the curriculum (as well as recommendations, essays, and interviews), which collectively offer a fuller picture of the applicant than does a grade-point average. Moreover, these schools point out that their students are often more motivated and proficient learners, thus better prepared for college, than their counterparts at traditional schools who have been preoccupied with grades.

In any case, college admission is surely no bar to eliminating grades in elementary and middle schools because colleges are largely indifferent to what students have done before high school. That leaves proponents of grades for younger children to fall back on some version of an argument I call "BGUTI": Better Get Used To It (Kohn, 2005). The claim here is that we should do unpleasant and unnecessary things to children now in order to prepare them for the fact that just such things will be done to them later. This justification is exactly as absurd as it sounds, yet it continues to drive education policy.

Even when administrators aren't ready to abandon traditional report cards, individual teachers can help to rescue learning in their own classrooms with a two-pronged strategy to "neuter grades," as one teacher described it. First, they can stop putting letter or number grades on individual assignments and instead offer only qualitative feedback. Report cards are bad enough, but the destructive effects reported by researchers (on interest in learning, preference for challenge, and quality of thinking) are compounded when students are rated on what they do in school day after day. Teachers can mitigate considerable harm by replacing grades with authentic assessments; moreover, as we've seen, any feedback they may already offer becomes much more useful in the absence of letter or number ratings.

Second, although teachers may be required to submit a final grade, there's no requirement for them to decide unilaterally what that grade will be. Thus, students can be invited to participate in that process either as a negotiation (such that the teacher has the final say) or by simply permitting students to grade themselves. If people find that idea alarming, it's probably because they realize it creates a more democratic classroom, one in which teachers must create a pedagogy and a curriculum that will truly engage students rather than allow teachers to coerce them into doing whatever they're told. In fact, negative reactions to this proposal ("It's unrealistic!") point up how grades function as a mechanism for controlling students rather than as a necessary or constructive way to report information about their performance.

I spoke recently to several middle and high school teachers who have degraded their classes. Jeff Robbins, who has taught eighth-grade science in New Jersey for fifteen years, concedes that "life was easier with grades" because they take so much less time than meaningful assessment. That efficiency came at a huge cost, though, he noticed: Kids were stressed out and also preferred to avoid intellectual risks. "They'll take an easier assignment that will guarantee the A."

Initially Robbins announced that any project or test could be improved and resubmitted for a higher grade. Unfortunately, that failed to address the underlying problem, and he eventually realized he had to stop grading entirely. Now, he offers comments to all of his 125 students "about what they're doing and what they need to improve on" and makes abbreviated notes in his grade book. At the end of the term, over a period of about a week, he grabs each student for a conversation at some point — "because the system isn't designed to allow kids this kind of feedback" — asking "what did you learn, how did you learn it. Only at the very end of the conversation [do] I ask what grade will reflect it . . . and we'll collectively arrive at something." Like many other teachers I've spoken to over the years, Robbins says he almost always accepts students' suggestions because they typically pick the same grade that he would have.

Jim Drier, an English teacher at Mundelein High School in Illinois who has about ninety students ranging "from at-risk to A.P.," was relieved to find that it "really doesn't take that long" to write at least a brief note on students' assignments — "a reaction to what they did and some advice on how they might improve." But he never gives them "a number or grade on anything they do. The things that grades make kids do are heartbreaking for an educator": arguing with teachers, fighting with parents, cheating, memorizing facts just for a test and then forgetting them. "This is not why I became a teacher."

Without grades, "I think my relationships with students are better," Drier says. "Their writing improves more quickly and the things they learn stay with them longer. I've had lots of kids tell me it's changed their attitude about coming to school." He expected resistance from parents but says that in three years only one parent has objected, and it may help that he sends a letter home to explain exactly what he's doing and why. Now two of his colleagues are joining him in eliminating grades.

Drier's final grades are based on students' written self-assessments, which, in turn, are based on their review of items in their portfolios. He meets with about three-quarters of them twice a term, in most cases briefly, to assess their performance and, if necessary (although it rarely happens) to discuss a concern about the grade they've suggested. Asked how he manages without a grade book full of letters or numbers, Drier replies, "If I spend eighteen weeks with them, I have a pretty good idea what their writing and reasoning ability is."

A key element of authentic assessment for these and other teachers is the opportunity for students to help design the assessment and reflect on its purposes — individually and as a class. Notice how different this is from the more common variant of self-assessment in which students merely monitor their progress toward the teacher's (or legislature's) goals and in which they must reduce their learning to numerical ratings with gradelike rubrics.

Points of overlap as well as divergence emerge from the testimonies of such teachers, some of which have been collected by Joe Bower (n.d.), an educator in Red Deer, Alberta. Some teachers, for example, *evaluate* their students' performance (in qualitative terms, of course), but others believe it's more constructive to offer only *feedback*—which is to say, information. On the latter view, "the alternative to grades is description" and "the starting point for description is a plain sheet of paper, not a form which leads and homogenizes description" (Marshall, 1968, pp. 131, 143).

Teachers also report a variety of reactions to de-grading not only from colleagues and administrators but also from the students themselves. John Spencer (2010), an Arizona middle school teacher, concedes that "many of the 'high performing' students were angry at first. They saw it as unfair. They viewed school as work and their peers as competitors. . . . Yet, over time they switch and they calm down. They end up learning more once they aren't feeling the pressure" from grades.

Indeed, research suggests that the common tendency of students to focus on grades doesn't reflect an innate predilection or a "learning style" to be accommodated; rather, it's due to having been led for years to work for grades. In one study (Butler, 1988), some students were encouraged to think about how well they performed at a creative task while others were just invited to be imaginative. Each student was then taken to a room that contained a pile of pictures that other people had drawn in response to the same instructions. It also contained some information that told them how to figure out their "creativity score." Sure enough, the children who were told to think about their performance now wanted to know how they had done relative to their peers; those who had been allowed to become immersed in the task were more interested in seeing *what* their peers had done.

Grades don't prepare children for the "real world"—unless one has in mind a world where interest in learning and quality of thinking are unimportant. Nor are grades a necessary part of schooling, any more than paddling or taking extended dictation could be described that way. Still, it takes courage to do right by kids in an era when the quantitative matters more than the qualitative, when meeting (someone else's) standards counts for more than exploring ideas, and when anything "rigorous" is automatically assumed to be valuable. We have to be willing to challenge the conventional wisdom, which in this case means asking not how to improve grades but how to jettison them once and for all.

REFERENCES

Anderman, E. M., & Murdock, T. B., eds. (2007). *Psychology of academic cheating.* Burlington, MA: Elsevier Academic Press.

Bedell, J. (2010, July). Blog post, available at www.joebower.org/2010/07/grading-moratorium-jason-bedell.html.

Bower, J. (2010, March 28). Blog post, available at www.joebower.org/2010/03/detoxing-students-from-grade-use.html.

Bower, J. (n.d.). Blog post, available at www.joebower.org/p/grading-moratorium.html.

Butler, R. (1988). Enhancing and undermining intrinsic motivation: The effects of task-involving and ego-involving evaluation on interest and performance. *British Journal of Educational Psychology 58,* 1–14.

Crooks, A. D. (1933). Marks and marking systems: A digest. *Journal of Educational Research 27*(4), 259–72.

De Zouche, D. (1945). "The wound *is* mortal": Marks, honors, unsound activities. *The Clearing House 19*(6), 339–44.

Eisner, E. W. (2001, Jan.). What does it mean to say a school is doing well? *Phi Delta Kappan,* pp. 367–72.

Gardner, H. (1991). *The unschooled mind: How children think and how schools should teach.* New York: Basic Books.

Grolnick, W. S., & Ryan, R .M. (1987). Autonomy in children's learning: An experimental and individual difference investigation. *Journal of Personality and Social Psychology 52,* 890–98.

Kirschenbaum, H., Simon, S. B., & Napier, R. W. (1971). *Wad-ja-get?: The grading game in American education.* New York: Hart.

Kohn, A. (1999a). *Punished by rewards: The trouble with gold stars, incentive plans, A's, praise, and other bribes.* Rev. ed. Boston: Houghton Mifflin.

Kohn, A. (1999b). *The schools our children deserve: Moving beyond traditional classrooms and "tougher standards."* Boston: Houghton Mifflin.

Kohn, A. (1999c, March). From degrading to de-grading. *High School Magazine,* pp. 38–43.

Kohn, A. (2001, Sept. 26). Beware of the standards, not just the tests. *Education Week,* pp. 52, 38.

Kohn, A. (2005, Sept. 7). Getting hit on the head lessons. *Education Week*, pp. 52, 46–47.

Kohn, A. (2006, March). The trouble with rubrics. *Language Arts*, pp. 12–15.

Linder, I. H. (1940, July). Is there a substitute for teachers' grades? *School Board Journal*, pp. 25, 26, 79.

Maehr, M. L., & Midgley, C. (1996). *Transforming school cultures*. Boulder, CO: Westview.

Marshall, M. S. (1968). *Teaching without grades*. Corvallis, OR: Oregon State University Press.

Mathews, J. (2006, Nov. 14). Just whose idea was all this testing? *Washington Post*.

McNeil, L. M. (1986). *Contradictions of control: School structure and school knowledge*. New York: Routledge & Kegan Paul.

Milton, O., Pollio, H. R., & Eison, J. A. (1986). *Making sense of college grades*. San Francisco: Jossey-Bass.

Neill, M., Bursh, P., Schaeffer, B., Thall, C., Yohe, M., & Zappardino, P. (1995). *Implementing performance assessments: A guide to classroom, school, and system reform*. Cambridge, MA: FairTest.

Nicholls, J. G., & Hazzard, S. P. (1993). *Education as adventure: Lessons from the second grade*. New York: Teachers College Press.

Olson, K. (2006, Nov. 8). The wounds of schooling. *Education Week*, pp. 28–29.

Pulfrey, C., Buch, C., & Butera, F. (2011). Why grades engender performance-avoidance goals: The mediating role of autonomous motivation. *Journal of Educational Psychology 103*, 683–700.

Spencer, J. (2010, July). Blog post, available at www.joebower.org/2010/07/grading-moratorium-john-spencer.html.

White, C. B., & Fantone, J. C. (2010). Pass-fail grading: Laying the foundation for self-regulated learning. *Advances in Health Science Education 15*, 469–77.

Wilson, M. (2006). *Rethinking rubrics in writing assessment*. Portsmouth, NH: Heinemann.

Wilson, M. (2009, Nov). Responsive writing assessment. *Educational Leadership*, pp. 58–62.

CHAPTER 9

Schooling Beyond Measure

As we tend to value the results of education for their measurableness, so we tend to undervalue and at last ignore those results which are too intrinsically valuable to be measured.

**—Edmond G. A. Holmes, chief inspector of
elementary schools for Great Britain, 1911**

The reason that standardized test results tend to be so uninformative and misleading is closely related to the reason that these tests are so popular in the first place. That, in turn, is connected to our attraction to—and the trouble with—grades, rubrics, and various practices commended to us as "data-based."

The common denominator? Our culture's worshipful regard for numbers. Roger Jones, a physicist, called it "the heart of our modern idolatry . . . the belief that the quantitative description of things is paramount and even complete in itself."

Quantification can be entertaining, of course: Readers love top-ten lists, and our favorite parts of the news are those with numerical components— sports, business, and weather. There's something comforting about the simplicity of specificity. As the educator Selma Wassermann observed, "Numbers help to relieve the frustrations of the unknown, for nothing feels more certain or gives greater security than a number." If the numbers are get-

"Schooling Beyond Measure" was originally published in Education Week *on September 19, 2012. This is a slightly expanded version of the published article.*

ting larger over time, we figure we must be making progress. Anything that resists being reduced to numerical terms, by contrast, seems vaguely suspicious, or at least suspiciously vague.

In his book *Trust in Numbers*, historian Theodore Porter points out that quantification has long exerted a particular attraction for Americans. "The systematic use of IQ tests to classify students, opinion polls to quantify the public mood . . .[and] even cost-benefit analyses to assess public works — all in the name of impersonal objectivity — are distinctive products of . . . American culture."

In calling this sensibility into question, I'm not denying that there's a place for quantification. Rather, I'm pointing out that it doesn't always seem to know its place. If the question is "How tall is he?" "six-foot-two" is a more useful answer than "pretty damn tall." But what if the question were "Is that a good city to live in?" or "How does she feel about her sister?" or "Would you rather have your child in this teacher's classroom or that one's?"

The habit of looking for numerical answers to just about *any* question can probably be traced back to overlapping academic traditions like behaviorism and scientism (the belief that all true knowledge is scientific), as well as the arrogance of economists or statisticians who think their methods can be applied to everything in life. The resulting overreliance on numbers is, ironically, based more on faith than on reason. And the results can be disturbing.

In education, the question "How do we assess (kids, teachers, schools)?" has morphed over the years into "How do we measure . . . ?" We've forgotten that assessment doesn't require measurement — and, moreover, that the most valuable forms of assessment are often qualitative (say, a narrative account of a child's progress by an observant teacher who knows the child well) rather than quantitative (a standardized test score). Yet the former may well be brushed aside in favor of the latter — by people who don't even bother to ask what was *on* the test. It's a number, so we sit up and pay attention. Over time, the more data we accumulate, the less we really know.

You've heard it said that tests and other measures are, like technology, merely neutral tools, and all that matters is what we do with the information? Baloney. The measure affects that which is measured. Indeed, the fact that we chose to measure in the first place carries causal weight. His speechwriters had President George W. Bush proclaim, "Measurement is the cornerstone of learning." What they should have written was, "Measurement is the cornerstone of the kind of learning that lends itself to being measured."

One example: It's easier to score a student writer's proficiency with sentence structure than her proficiency at evoking excitement in a reader. Thus, the introduction of a scoring device like a rubric will likely lead to more emphasis on teaching mechanics. Either that, or the notion of "evocative" writing will be flattened into something that can be expressed as a numerical rating. Objectivity has a way of objectifying. Pretty soon the question of what our whole education system ought to be doing gives way to the question of which educational goals are easiest to measure. That means, in the words of University of Colorado professor Kenneth Howe, putting "the quest for accurate measurement—and control—above the quest for educationally and morally defensible policies."

A few years ago, a writer in *Education Week* recalled a conversation with the director of testing for a state's education system who "agreed that being able to make a public presentation was likely to be a more important skill for adults than knowing how to factor a polynomial. 'But,' he added, 'I know how to test the ability to factor a polynomial.'" Only the latter, therefore, was going to be assessed—and therefore taught.

I'll say it again: Quantification does have a role to play. We need to be able to count how many kids are in each class if we want to know the effects of class size. But the effects of class size on what? Will we look only at test scores, ignoring outcomes such as students' enthusiasm about learning or their experience of the classroom as a caring community?

Too much is lost to us—or warped—as a result of our love affair with numbers. And there are other casualties as well:

1. *We miss the forest while counting the trees.* Rigorous ratings of how well something is being done tend to distract us from asking whether that activity is sensible or ethical. Dubious cultural values and belief systems are often camouflaged by numerical precision, sometimes out to several decimal places. Stephen Jay Gould, in his book *The Mismeasure of Man*, provided ample evidence that meretricious findings are often produced by impressively meticulous quantifiers.

2. *We become obsessed with winning.* An infatuation with numbers not only emerges from but also exacerbates our cultural addiction to competition. It's easier to know how many others we've beaten, and by how much, if achievements have been quantified. But once they're quantified, it's tempting for us to spend our time comparing and ranking—trying to triumph over one another rather than cooperating.

3. *We deny our subjectivity.* Sometimes the exclusion of what's hard to quantify is rationalized on the grounds that it's "merely subjective." But subjectivity isn't purged by relying on numbers; it's just driven underground, yielding the *appearance* of objectivity. An "86" at the top of a paper is steeped in the teacher's subjective criteria just as much as his comments about that paper. Even a score on a math quiz isn't "objective": It reflects the teacher's choices about how many and what type of questions to include, how difficult they should be, how much each answer will count, and so on. Ditto for standardized tests — except the people making those choices are distant and invisible.

Subjectivity isn't a bad thing; it's about judgment, which is a marvelous human capacity that, in the plural, supplies the lifeblood of a democratic society. What's bad is the use of numbers to pretend that we've eliminated it.

Skepticism about — and denial of — judgment in general is compounded these days by an institutionalized distrust of *teachers'* judgments. Hence the tidal wave of standardized testing in the name of "accountability." Part of the point is to bypass the teachers, and indeed to evaluate them, too. The exalted status of numerical data also helps to explain why teachers are increasingly being trained rather than educated.

Interestingly, some thinkers in the business world understand all of this. The late W. Edwards Deming, guru of quality management, once declared, "The most important things we need to manage can't be measured." If that's true of what we need to manage, it should be even more obvious that it's true of what we need to teach.

It should be, but it isn't. As a result, we're left vulnerable to the misuse of numbers, a timely example being the pseudoscience of "value-added modeling" of test data — debunked by experts but continuing to sucker the credulous. The trouble, however, isn't limited to lying with statistics. Quantification can be a problem even when it's done honestly and competently. Better tests — or tests that are formative rather than summative — won't solve the problem. Neither will rating based on more ambitious or humanistic criteria.

At the surface, yes, we're obliged to do something about bad tests and poorly designed rubrics and meaningless data. But what lies underneath is an irrational attachment to tests, rubrics, and data, per se — or, more precisely, our penchant for reducing to numbers what is distorted by that very act.

CHAPTER 10

Turning Children into Data
A Skeptic's Guide to
Assessment Programs

Not everything that counts can be counted, and not everything that can be counted counts.

—Albert Einstein

Programs with generic-sounding names that offer techniques for measuring (and raising) student achievement have been sprouting like fungi in a rain forest: "Learning Focused Schools," "Curriculum-Based Measurements," "Professional Learning Communities," and many others whose names include "data," "progress," or "RTI." Perhaps you've seen their ads in education periodicals. Perhaps you've pondered the fact that they can *afford* these ads, presumably because of how much money they've already collected from struggling school districts.

When I'm asked about one of these programs, I have to confess that I just can't keep up with every new stall that opens in this bazaar—and the same is true of the neighboring marketplace that's packed with discipline and classroom management programs. (Hint: Here, extreme skepticism is warranted whenever the name includes the word "behavior.") Still, it is possible to sketch some criteria for judging any given program—preferably *before* someone requests a purchase order.

"Turning Children into Data: A Skeptic's Guide to Assessment Programs" was originally published in Education Week *on August 25, 2010.*

So let's imagine that your community is buzzing about something called ABA: "Achievement-Based Assessment"—or, perhaps, "Assessment-Based Achievement"—whose website boasts of "monitoring and improving each student's learning with proven data-focused strategies."

Worth a try? Well, we certainly can't decide on the basis of how ABA markets itself. Just about any descriptor that might seem appealing, even progressive, has been co-opted by now: Every outfit claims to help teachers "collaborate" in order to focus on the "learning" (rather than just the teaching) as they look at "authentic" outcomes and "differentiate" the instruction with a "developmental" approach that emphasizes "critical (or higher-order) thinking" skills—in order to prepare your students for—raise your hand if you saw this coming—the "21st century."

Obviously we're going to have to look a little deeper and ask a few pointed questions.

1. *What is its basic conception of assessment?* To get a sense of how well things are going and where help is needed, we ought to focus on the actual learning that students do over a period of time—ideally, deep learning that consists of more than practicing skills and memorizing facts. If you agree, then you'd be very skeptical about a program that relies on discrete, contrived, testlike assessments. You'd object to any procedure that seems mechanical, in which standardized protocols like rubrics supplant teachers' professional judgments based on personal interaction with their students. And the only thing worse than "benchmark" tests (tests in between the tests) would be computerized monitoring tools, which reading expert Richard Allington has succinctly characterized as "idiotic."

2. *What is its goal?* Ask not only what the program is but why it exists—and, specifically, whether its *raison d'être* is not to help kids understand ideas and become thoughtful questioners but merely to raise their scores on standardized tests. (Elsewhere, I've reviewed evidence showing not only that these tests are completely inadequate for assessing important intellectual proficiencies but also that high scores are actually correlated with a superficial approach to learning.) Obviously, anyone who harbors doubts about the validity or value of standardized tests wouldn't want to have anything to do with a program that's designed mostly with them in mind.

3. *Does it reduce everything to numbers?* If all the earnest talk about "data" (in the context of educating children) doesn't make you at least a little bit uneasy, it's time to recharge your crap detector. Most assessment systems are based on an outdated behaviorist model that assumes nearly everything can — and should — be quantified. But the more educators allow themselves to be turned into accountants, the more trivial their teaching becomes and the more their assessments miss.

That's why I was heartened recently to receive a note describing how some teachers on a Midwestern high school's improvement team took a long, hard look at the Professional Learning Communities model and said no thanks. They were put off by its designers' frank admiration of for-profit corporations as well as its "misguided premise that every subject area can be broken down into core concepts which then have to be quantified." The teachers understood that learning doesn't have to be measured in order to be assessed. And they feared that "true learning and engagement" — along with a commitment to be "responsive to students' needs [and] lives" — might be lost.

These teachers ultimately decided to reject the technocratic PLC approach in favor of an alternative they designed themselves. It focused on teachers' personal "connection[s] with our subject area" as the basis for helping students to think "like mathematicians or historians or writers or scientists, instead of drilling them in the vocabulary of those subject areas or breaking down the skills." In a word, the teachers put kids before data.

Of course, this powerful exercise in professional development never would have happened if the administration had simply imposed PLCs (or a similar program) on the teachers, treating them like technicians who merely carry out orders. Which brings us to . . .

4. Is it about "doing to" or "working with"? Steer clear of any program whose curriculum or assessments are so structured, so prescriptive and prefabricated, that teachers lack any real autonomy. By now we ought to know that systems intended to be "teacher-proof" are not only disrespectful but chimerical: They are the perpetual-motion machines of education. One sure sign of disrespect is the use of incentives or sanctions to make teachers get with the program, including compensation that hinges on compliance or on some measure of student achievement. All that does is corrupt the measure (unless it's a test score, in which case it's already misleading), undermine collaboration among teachers, and make teaching less joyful and therefore less effective by meaningful criteria.

Likewise, you'd want to make sure that *students'* autonomy is respected since kids should have a lot to say about their assessment. If they feel controlled, then even a cleverly designed program is unlikely to have a constructive effect. Again, any use of carrots and sticks should set off alarms. As Jerome Bruner once said, we want to create an environment where students can "experience success and failure not as reward and punishment but as information." That pretty much rules out grades or similar ratings.

5. *Is its priority to support kids' interest?* In attempting to track and boost achievement, do we damage what's most critical to long-term quality of learning: students' *desire* to learn? It's disturbing if a program is so preoccupied with data and narrowly defined skills that it doesn't even bother to talk about this issue. More important, look at the real-world effects: Once a school adopts the program, are kids more excited about what they're doing — or has learning been made to feel like drudgery?

6. *Does it avoid excessive assessment?* The more that students are led to focus on how well they're doing, the less engaged they tend to become with *what* they're doing. Instead of stuff they want to figure out, the curriculum just becomes stuff at which they're required to get better. A school that's all about achievement and performance is a school that's not really about discovery and understanding.

While some education conferences are genuinely inspiring, others serve mostly to demonstrate how even intelligent educators can be remarkably credulous, nodding agreeably at descriptions of programs that ought to elicit fury or laughter, avidly copying down hollow phrases from a consultant's PowerPoint presentation, awed by anything that's borrowed from the business world or involves digital technology.

Many companies and consultants thrive on this credulity, and also on teachers' isolation, fatalism, and fear (of demands by clueless officials to raise test scores at any cost). With a good dose of critical thinking and courage, a willingness to say "This is bad for kids and we won't have any part of it," we could drive these outfits out of business — and begin to take back our schools.

CHAPTER 11

Whoever Said There's No Such Thing as a Stupid Question Never Looked Carefully at a Standardized Test

It can't be repeated often enough: Standardized tests are very poor measures of the intellectual capabilities that matter most, and that's true because of how they're designed, not just because of how they're used. Like other writers, I've relied on arguments and research to make this point. But sometimes a telling example can be more effective. So here's an item that appeared on the state high school math exam in Massachusetts:

$$n \quad 1 \quad 2 \quad 3 \quad 4 \quad 5 \quad 6$$
$$t_n \quad 3 \quad 5 \quad \underline{\ }\ \underline{\ }\ \underline{\ }\ \underline{\ }$$

The first two terms of a sequence, t_1 and t_2, are shown above as 3 and 5. Using the rule: $t_n = (t_{n-1})$ plus (t_{n-2}), where n is greater than or equal to 3, complete the table.

If (a) your reaction to this question was "Huh?" (or "Uh-oh. What's with the teeny little n's?") and (b) you lead a reasonably successful and satisfying life, it may be worth pausing to ask why we deny diplomas to high school students just because they, too, struggle with such questions. Hence [Deborah] Meier's Mandate: "No student should be expected to meet an

"Whoever Said There's No Such Thing as a Stupid Question Never Looked Carefully at a Standardized Test" was originally published as a blog post on September 16, 2011.

academic requirement that a cross section of successful adults in the community cannot."

But perhaps you figured out that the test designers are just asking you to add 3 and 5 to get 8, then add 5 and 8 to get 13, then add 8 to 13 to get 21, and so on. If so, congratulations. But what is the question really testing? A pair of math educators, Al Cuoco and Faye Ruopp, pointed out how much less is going on here than meets the eye:

> The problem simply requires the ability to follow a rule; there is no mathematics in it at all. And many 10th-grade students will get it wrong, not because they lack the mathematical thinking necessary to fill in the table, but simply because they haven't had experience with the notation. Next year, however, teachers will prep students on how to use formulas like $t_n = t_{n-1} + t_{n-2}$, more students will get it right, and state education officials will tell us that we are increasing mathematical literacy.[1]

In contrast to most criticisms of standardized testing, which look at tests in the aggregate and their effects on entire populations, this is a bottom-up critique. Its impact is to challenge not only the view that such tests provide "objective" data about learning but to jolt us into realizing that high scores are not necessarily good news and low scores are not necessarily bad news.

If the questions on a test measure little more than the ability to apply an algorithm mindlessly, then you can't use the results of that test to make pronouncements about this kid's (or this school's, or this state's, or this country's) proficiency at mathematical thinking. Similarly, if the questions on a science or social studies test mostly gauge the number of dates or definitions that have been committed to memory — and, perhaps, a generic skill at taking tests — it would be foolish to draw conclusions about students' understanding of those fields.

A parallel bottom-up critique emerges from interviewing children about why they picked the answers they did on multiple-choice exams — answers for which they received no credit — and discovering that some of their reasons are actually quite sophisticated, which of course one would never know just by counting the number of their "correct" answers.[2]

No newspaper, no politician, no parent or school administrator should ever assume that a test score is a valid and meaningful indicator without looking carefully at the questions on that test to ascertain that they're designed to measure something of importance and do so effectively. Moreover, as Cuoco and Ruopp remind us, *rising* scores over time are often nothing to cheer about because the kind of instruction intended to prepare kids for the test — even when it does so successfully — may be instruction that's not particularly valuable. Indeed, teaching designed to raise test scores typically reduces the time available for real learning. And it's naïve to tell teachers they should "just teach well and let the tests take care of themselves." Indeed, if the questions on the tests are sufficiently stupid, bad teaching may produce better scores than good teaching.

NOTES

1. Cuoco and Ruopp, "Math Exam Rationale Doesn't Add Up," *Boston Globe*, May 24, 1998: D3.

2. For examples (and analysis) of this kind of discrepancy, see Banesh Hoffmann, *The Tyranny of Testing* (New York: Crowell-Collier, 1962); Deborah Meier, "Why Reading Tests Don't Test Reading," *Dissent*, Fall 1981: 457–66; Walt Haney and Laurie Scott, "Talking with Children About Tests: An Exploratory Study of Test Item Ambiguity," in Roy O. Freedle and Richard P. Duran, eds., *Cognitive and Linguistic Analyses of Test Performance* (Norwood, NJ: Ablex, 1987); and Clifford Hill and Eric Larsen, *Children and Reading Tests* (Stamford, CT: Ablex, 2000).

CHAPTER 12

Why the Best Teachers Don't Give Tests

Frankly, I'm baffled by the number of educators who are adamantly opposed to standardized testing yet raise no objection to other practices that share important features with such testing.

For starters, consider those lists of specific, prescriptive curriculum standards to which the tests are yoked. Here we find the same top-down control and one-size-fits-all mentality that animate standardized testing. Yet from the early days of the "accountability" movement right down to current efforts to impose the Gates-funded Common Core from coast to coast, an awful lot of people give the standards (and the whole *idea* of uniform standards) a pass while frowning only at the exams used to enforce them.[1]

Example 2: Elaborate rubrics used to judge students' performance represent another form of standardized assessment that's rarely recognized as such. The point is to break down something, such as a piece of writing, into its parts so that teachers, and sometimes the students themselves, can rate each of them, the premise being that it's both possible and desirable for all readers to arrive at the same number for each criterion. Rubrics are borne of a demand to quantify and an impulse to simplify. One result, argues Maja Wilson, is that "the standardization of the rubric produces standardized writers."[2] But, again, even many teachers who are outraged by standardized tests don't blink when standardization is smuggled in through the back door. Some insist, against all evidence to the contrary, that there's no problem as long as one uses a *good* rubric.

"Why the Best Teachers Don't Give Tests" was originally published as a blog post on October 31, 2014.

It's my third example, though, on which I'd like to linger. When teachers test their students, the details of those tests will differ from one classroom to the next, which means these assessments by definition are not standardized and can't be used to compare students across schools or states. But they're still tests, and as a result they're still limited and limiting.

As with rubrics (and grades), there's a reflexive tendency to insist that we just need *better* tests, or that we ought to just modify the way they're administered (for example, by allowing students to retake them). And, yes, it's certainly true that some are worse than others. Multiple-choice tests are uniquely flawed as assessments for exactly the same reason that multiple-choice standardized tests are: They're meant to trick students who understand the concepts into picking the wrong answer, and they don't allow kids to generate, or even explain, their responses. Multiple-choice exams can be clever, but as test designer Roger Farr of Indiana University ultimately concluded, there is no way "to build a multiple choice question that allows students to show what they can do with what they know."

We can also concede that some *reasons* for giving tests are more problematic than others. There's a difference between using them to figure out who needs help—or, for more thoughtful teachers, what aspects of their own instruction may have been ineffective—and using them to compel students to pay attention and complete their assignments. In the latter case, a test is employed to pressure kids to do what they have little interest in doing. Rather than address possible deficiencies in one's curriculum or pedagogy (say, the exclusion of students from any role in making decisions about what they'll learn), one need only sound a warning about an upcoming test—or, in an even more blatant exercise of power, surprise students with a pop quiz—to elicit compliance.

Even allowing for variation in the design of the tests and the motives of the testers, however, the bottom line is that these instruments are typically more about measuring the number of facts that have been crammed into students' short-term memories than they are about assessing understanding.[3] Tests, including those that involve essays, are part of a traditional model of instruction in which information is transmitted to students (by means of lectures and textbooks) so that it can be disgorged later on command. That's why it's so disconcerting to find teachers who are proud of their student-centered approach to instruction, who embrace active and interactive forms of learning, yet continue to rely on tests as the primary, or even sole, form of assessment in their classrooms.

While some of their questions may require problem-solving skills, tests, per se, are artificial pencil-and-paper exercises that measure how much students remember and how good they are at the discrete skill of taking tests. That's how it's possible for a student to be a talented thinker and yet score poorly. Most teachers can, without hesitation, name several such students in their classes when the exams are designed by Pearson or ETS but may fail to see that the same thing applies in the case of performance on tests they design themselves.

Not only do tests assess the intellectual proficiencies that matter least, however — they also have the potential to alter students' goals and the way they approach learning. The more you're led to focus on what you're going to have to know for a test, the less likely you are to plunge into a story or engage fully with the design of a project or experiment. And intellectual immersion can be all but smothered if those tests are given, or even talked about, frequently. Learning in order to pass a test is qualitatively different from learning for its own sake.[4]

Many years ago, the eminent University of Chicago educator Philip Jackson interviewed fifty teachers who had been identified as exceptional at their craft. Among his findings was a consistent lack of emphasis on testing, if not a deliberate decision to minimize the practice, on the part of these teachers.[5] The first reason for this, I think, is that exemplary educators understand that tests are not a particularly useful form of assessment. Second, though, these teachers learned at some point that they didn't *need* tests. The most impressive classrooms and curricula are designed to help the teacher know as much as possible about how students are making sense of things. When kids are engaged in meaningful, active learning — for example, designing extended, interdisciplinary projects — teachers who watch and listen as those projects are being planned and carried out have access to, and actively interpret, a continuous stream of information about what each student is able to do and where he or she requires help. It would be superfluous to give students a test after the learning is done. We might even say that the more a teacher is inclined to use a test to gauge student progress, the more that tells us something is wrong — perhaps with the extent of the teacher's informal and informed observation, perhaps with the quality of the tasks, perhaps with the whole model of learning. If, for example, the teacher favors direct instruction, he or she probably won't have much idea what's going on in the students' minds. That will lead naturally to the conclusion that a test is "necessary" to gauge how they're doing.[6]

Assessment literally means to sit beside, and that's just what our most thoughtful educators urge us to do. Yetta Goodman coined the compound noun "kidwatching" to describe reading with each child to gauge his or her proficiency. Marilyn Burns insists that one-on-one conversations tell us far more about students' mathematical understanding than a test ever could — since all wrong answers aren't alike. Of course this assumes that we're really interested in kids' understanding, not merely their level of phonemic awareness or ability to apply an algorithm. The less ambitious one's educational goals, the more likely that a test will suffice — and that the words *testing* and *assessing* will be used interchangeably.

One can fill a bookshelf with accounts of other forms of authentic assessment: portfolios, culminating projects, performance assessments, and what the late Ted Sizer called "exhibitions of mastery": opportunities for students to demonstrate their proficiency not by recalling facts on demand but by *doing* something: constructing and conducting (and explaining the results of) an experiment, creating a restaurant menu in a foreign language, turning a story into a play. In other words, when some form of evaluation is desired after, rather than during, the learning, tests *still* aren't necessary or even particularly helpful. They needn't be used for "summative," let alone for "formative," assessment.

Many of us rail against standardized tests not only because of the harmful uses to which they're put but because they're imposed on us. It's more unsettling to acknowledge that the tests we come up with ourselves can also be damaging. The good news is that far superior alternatives are available.

NOTES

1. See my essay "Beware of the Standards, Not Just the Tests," *Education Week*, September 26, 2001 — available at www.alfiekohn.org/article/ beware-standards-just-tests.

   This phenomenon is even more pronounced in Canada. Its education system is completely decentralized; each province controls its own policies. Despite the considerable variation in the amount of testing from one to the next, however, all of the provinces have very specific grade-by-grade curricula that every teacher is expected to teach. Objections to this level of control, with the concomitant diminution of autonomy for teachers, are rarely heard — even in provinces where there is outspoken resistance to testing.

2. Maja Wilson, *Rethinking Rubrics in Writing Assessment* (Heinemann, 2006), p. 39.

3. A spate of recent studies that attracted considerable attention in the popular press argues that frequent tests (including self-tests) are more effective than other forms of studying. But the outcome measure in these studies is almost always limited to the number of facts that are correctly recalled on later tests. Rather than offering an argument in favor of conventional assessment, these experiments actually illuminate how words like "learning" and "achievement" — as used by researchers and journalists alike — often mean little more than the successful, and presumably temporary, process of memorizing facts. For a close look at one such study, see chapter 22.

4. I recently made this point — about how the anticipation of being tested can distract students from engaging with ideas — in a Twitter post that was retweeted more than 400 times. This degree of popularity led me to suspect I had been misunderstood. I followed up with a clarification that *all* tests have this effect, not just standardized tests. The retweet rate dropped off by 90 percent.

5. Philip W. Jackson, *Life in Classrooms* (Teachers College Press, 1968/1990).

6. Frank Smith once wrote, "A teacher who cannot tell without a test whether a student is learning should not be in the classroom" (*Insult to Intelligence* [Heinemann, 1986], p. 259). I see what he means, but his formulation strikes me as a bit harsh. Teachers need help to learn how to assess without tests, and they need support and encouragement to eliminate a practice that is still used by most of their colleagues and widely expected by administrators, parents, and the students themselves. Moreover, the barrier to gauging how successfully students are learning often lies not with the teacher but with features of the school structure, such as classes that are too large or periods that are too short. That's an argument for organizing to change these problematic policies, not for continuing to test.

PART 3

In the Classroom

CHAPTER 13

A Dozen Essential Guidelines for Educators

To create the schools our children deserve, it's probably not necessary to devise specific policies and practices for every occasion. Rather, these will follow logically from a few core principles that we devise together. Here's a sample list of such principles, intended to start a conversation among educators, parents, and (let's not forget) the students themselves.

1. Learning should be organized around *problems*, *projects*, and (students') *questions*—not around lists of facts or skills, or separate disciplines.

2. Thinking is messy; deep thinking is really messy. Therefore beware prescriptive standards and outcomes that are too specific and orderly.

3. The primary criterion for what we do in schools: How will this affect kids' *interest* in the topic (and their excitement about learning more generally)?

4. If students are "off task," the problem may be with the task, not with the kids.

5. In outstanding classrooms, teachers do more listening than talking, and students do more talking than listening. Terrific teachers often have teeth marks on their tongues.

"A Dozen Essential Guidelines for Educators" was originally published as a blog post on October 29, 2013.

6. Children learn how to make good decisions by making decisions, not by following directions.

7. When we aren't sure how to solve a problem relating to curriculum, pedagogy, or classroom conflict, the best response is often to ask the kids.

8. The more focused we are on kids' "behaviors," the more we end up missing the kids themselves—along with the needs, motives, and reasons that underlie their actions.

9. If students are rewarded or praised for doing something (e.g., reading, solving problems, being kind), they'll likely lose interest in whatever they had to do to get the reward.

10. The more that students are led to focus on how well they're doing in school, the less engaged they'll tend to be with *what* they're doing in school.

11. All learning can be assessed, but the most important kinds of learning are very difficult to *measure*—and the quality of that learning may diminish if we try to reduce it to numbers.

12. Standardized tests assess the proficiencies that matter least. Such tests serve mostly to make unimpressive forms of instruction appear successful.

CHAPTER 14

What We Don't Know About Our Students—and Why

There's a scene near the beginning of *Small Change* (also known as *Pocket Money*), Truffaut's übercharming movie about children of all ages, in which a teacher makes each of her students recite a passage from a Molière play—a test of both memory and dramatic skill. The teacher is especially tough on one boy who chants the lines in a leaden monotone: She stands next to his desk and threatens (in front of his peers) to keep making him repeat the lines until his performance is to her liking. Abruptly, though, she is called away, and the moment she's gone, the boy comes to life. He stands up and begins to wander around the room while delivering the Molière monologue with remarkable power and spontaneity, revealing to his peers his considerable talents as an actor.

The point, of course, is to remind us adults how little we really know our kids and what they're capable of doing. That was a lesson I personally learned some years ago when I was teaching high school. I gave a ride one day to a fifteen-year-old girl, a student of mine who had no apparent interest in anything that I—or, from what I could gather, any of my colleagues—was teaching. Awkward and taciturn as usual that afternoon, she spoke only to ask if I would turn on the car radio, at which point she proceeded to sing along with every song that came on for the duration of the ride, displaying not only more enthusiasm than I had thought possible but also an astonishing gift for recall.

"What We Don't Know About Our Students—and Why" was originally published as a blog post on September 7, 2011.

Thinking back on this incident, I'm struck not only by what she did but by how I reacted. In relating the event to my colleagues the following day, I shook my head and smiled condescendingly at how this girl, a washout in the classroom, had evidently taken the time to learn pop lyrics to perfection. I mean, talk about misplaced priorities!

Only much later did it dawn on me that this student had something to teach me — about why her talent came as a complete surprise to me, and also about motivation and its relationship to achievement. If I (and her other teachers) had never seen her steel-trap memory in action or witnessed the look of total absorption I glimpsed in the car that day, that was undoubtedly because we hadn't taken enough time or shown enough interest so that she felt sufficiently safe to reveal who she was and what mattered to her.

And why wasn't she engaged in the classroom? Well, people tend to become more enthusiastic and proficient when they're in charge of what they're doing. How much choice had she been given about her schooling — not only the broad curriculum but the daily details of classroom life? Indeed, I had fallen back on grades to induce my students to do what I hadn't been able to help them find meaningful in its own right. This girl had chosen to learn those songs; no one had to promise her an A for doing so, or threaten her with an F for messing up. Her impressive achievement did not require carrots and sticks. In fact, it probably required their absence.

It was particularly disconcerting for me to realize that when the priorities of adults and kids diverge, we simply assume that ours ought to displace theirs. Stop wasting your time learning song lyrics when you could be doing important stuff — namely, whatever's in our lesson plans: solving for x or using apostrophes correctly or reading about the Crimean War. We tell more than we ask; we direct more than we listen; we use our power to pressure or even punish students whose interests don't align with ours. This has any number of unfortunate results, including loss of both self-confidence and interest in learning. But let's not forget to number among the sad consequences the fact that many students quite understandably choose to keep the important parts of themselves hidden from us. That's a shame in its own right, and it also prevents us from being the best teachers we can be.

CHAPTER 15

The Trouble with Calls for Universal "High-Quality" Pre-K

Universal pre-kindergarten education finally seems to be gathering momentum. President Obama highlighted the issue in his 2013 State of the Union address and then mentioned it again in 2014. Numerous states and cities are launching or expanding early-education initiatives, and New York City Mayor Bill de Blasio has made this his signature issue. Disagreements persist about the details of funding, but a real consensus has begun to develop that all young children deserve what has until now been unaffordable by low-income families.

But here's the catch: Very few people are talking about the *kind* of education that would be offered—other than declaring it should be "high quality." And that phrase is often interpreted to mean "high intensity": an accelerated version of skills-based teaching that most early-childhood experts regard as terrible. Poor children, as usual, tend to get the worst of this.

It doesn't bode well that many supporters of universal pre-K seem to be more concerned about economic imperatives than about what's good for kids. In 2013, for example, the president introduced the topic by emphasizing the need to "start at the earliest possible age" to "equip our citizens with the skills and training" they'll need in the workplace.[1] The *New York Times*, meanwhile, editorialized about how we must "tightly integrate the [pre-K] program with kindergarten through third grade so that 4-year-olds do not lose their momentum. It will have to prepare children well for the rigorous

---

"The Trouble with Calls for Universal 'High-Quality' Pre-K" was originally published as a blog post on February 1, 2014.

Common Core learning standards that promise to bring their math, science and literacy skills up to international norms."[2]

The top-down, test-driven regimen of Bush's "No Child Left Behind" and Obama's "Race to the Top" initiatives in K–12 education is now in the process of being nationalized with those Common Core standards championed by the *Times* — an enterprise largely funded, and relentlessly promoted, by corporate groups.[3] That same version of school reform, driven by an emphasis on global competitiveness and a determination to teach future workers as much as possible as soon as possible, would now be expanded to children who are barely out of diapers.

That doesn't leave much time for play. But even to the extent we want to promote meaningful *learning* in young children, the methods are likely to be counterproductive, featuring an emphasis on the direct instruction of skills and rote rehearsal of facts. This is the legacy of behaviorism: Children are treated as passive receptacles of knowledge, with few opportunities to investigate topics and pose questions that they find intriguing. In place of discovery and exploration, tots are trained to sit still and listen, to memorize lists of letters, numbers, and colors. Their success or failure is relentlessly monitored and quantified, and they're "reinforced" with stickers or praise for producing right answers and being compliant.

This dreary version of early-childhood education isn't just disrespectful of children; decades of research show it simply doesn't work well — and may even be damaging.[4] The same approach has long been over-represented in schools that serve low-income African American and Latino children, and it continues to find favor in inner-city charter schools, as I discuss in the following chapter. If we're not careful, calls to expand access to preschool will result in more of the same for younger children whose families can't afford an alternative.

Consider the basic equity argument. Proponents of universal pre-K cite research about the importance of early-life experiences, arguing that children in low-income families are at a real disadvantage in terms of intellectual stimulation, exposure to literacy, and so on. That disadvantage, they point out, can reverberate throughout their lives and is extremely difficult to reverse.

It is true that, on average, children in affluent homes hear more words spoken and have more books read to them. But, as Richard Rothstein points out, it's not just a matter of the number of words or books to which they're exposed so much as the *context* in which they're presented. "How parents

read to children is as important as whether they do, and an extensive literature confirms that more educated parents read aloud differently." Rather
than "sound[ing] out words or nam[ing] letters," these parents are more
likely to "ask questions that are creative, interpretive, or connective, such as,
'What do you think will happen next?' 'Does that remind you of what we did
yesterday?' Middle-class parents are more likely to read aloud to have fun, to
have conversations, or as an entree to the world outside. Their children learn
that reading is enjoyable."[5]

To oversimplify a bit, the homes of advantaged parents look more like
progressive schools, while the homes of disadvantaged parents look more
like back-to-basics, skills-oriented, traditional schools. It makes no sense to
try to send low-income children to preschools that intensify the latter approach, with rigorous drilling in letter-sound correspondences and number
recognition—the sort of instruction that turns learning into drudgery. As
Deborah Stipek, dean of Stanford's School of Education, once commented,
drill-and-skill instruction isn't how middle-class children got their edge, so
"why use a strategy to help poor kids catch up that didn't help middle class
kids in the first place?"[6]

Alas, that is precisely the strategy that tends to follow in the wake of
goals offered by most politicians and journalists who hold forth on education. If schooling is conceived as mostly an opportunity to train tomorrow's
employees, there's a tendency to look to behaviorist methods—despite the
fact that behaviorism has largely been discredited by experts in child development, cognition, and learning.

Lilian Katz, a leading authority in early-childhood education, once observed that we tend to "overestimate children academically and underesti-
mate them intellectually."[7] This is why a school that is exceedingly "rigorous"
can also be wholly unengaging, even sterile. If those who favor prescriptive
standards and high-stakes testing equate rigor with quality, it may be because they fail to distinguish between what is intellectual and what is merely
academic. The rarity of rich intellectual environments for young children
seems to leave only two possibilities, as Katz sees it: Either they spend their
time "making individual macaroni collages" or they're put to work to satisfy
"our quick-fix academic fervor."[8]

Happily, these do not exhaust the possibilities for early-childhood edu-
cation. One alternative is sketched out in a wonderful book by Katz and her
Canadian colleague Sylvia Chard called *Engaging Children's Minds: The Project
Approach* (3rd ed., Praeger, 2014). Here, teachers create extended studies of

rich themes that resonate with young children, such as babies, hospitals, or the weather. Children might spend a month learning about such a real-life topic, visiting, drawing, discussing, thinking.

And there are other, overlapping educational models, including two with Italian roots: Montessori education and the Reggio Emilia approach, where "young children are not marched or hurried sequentially from one different activity to the next, but instead encouraged to repeat key experiences, observe and re-observe, consider and reconsider, represent and re-represent."[9] Educators who have been influenced by Jean Piaget's discoveries about child development, meanwhile, have built on his recognition that children are active meaning makers who learn by constructing reality — intellectually, socially, and morally. One of my favorite practical resources in this vein for early-childhood educators is *Moral Classrooms, Moral Children* (2nd ed., Teacher's College Press, 2012) by the late Rheta DeVries and Betty Zan.

All of these approaches to educating young children offer opportunities to learn that are holistic and situated in a context. They take kids (and their questions) seriously, engage them as thinkers, and give them some say about what they're doing. The trouble is that current calls for "high-quality" universal pre-K are unlikely to produce learning opportunities that look anything like this — unless political activists begin to educate themselves about the nuances of education.

NOTES

1. See www.whitehouse.gov/the-press-office/2013/02/12/ remarks-president-state-union-address.

2. Editorial Board, *New York Times,* January 21, 2014: A18.

3. Some sample headlines in *Education Week*: "Business Executives Push Common Core Hard," "Business Groups Crank Up Defense of Common Core," "Chamber [of Commerce] President Calls for Support of Common Core in 2014." In 2009, Bill Gates defended the Common Core, a significant proportion of whose start-up costs have been paid by his foundation, for its capacity to eventually produce a "uniform base of customers." (See http://ow.ly/pxALx.)

4. Alfie Kohn, "Early Childhood Education: The Case Against Direct Instruction of Academic Skills," excerpted from *The Schools Our Children Deserve* (Boston: Houghton Mifflin, 1999), and available at www.alfiekohn.org/article/ early-childhood-education.

5. Richard Rothstein, "Class and the Classroom," *American School Board Journal*, October 2004, p. 18. For a description of newer research (by Kathryn Hirsh-Pasek and her colleagues) that confirms this insight, see Douglas Quenqua, "Quality of Words, Not Quantity, Is Crucial to Language Skills, Study Finds," *New York Times*, October 17, 2014: A22.

6. Stipek is quoted in David L. Kirp, "All My Children," *New York Times* Education Life, July 31, 2005: 21.

7. Lilian Katz, "What Can We Learn from Reggio Emilia?" In *The Hundred Languages of Children: The Reggio Emilia Approach to Early Childhood Education*, edited by Carolyn Edwards et al. (Norwood, NJ: Ablex, 1993), p. 31.

8. Lilian Katz, "The Disposition to Learn," *Principal*, May 1988: 16.

9. Carolyn Edwards, Lella Gandini, and George Forman, Introduction to *The Hundred Languages of Children*, op. cit., p. 7.

CHAPTER 16

Poor Teaching for Poor Children . . . in the Name of Reform

Love them or hate them, the proposals collectively known as "school reform" are mostly top-down policies: divert public money to quasi-private charter schools, pit states against one another in a race for federal education dollars, offer rewards when test scores go up, fire the teachers or close the schools when they don't.

Policy makers and the general public have paid much less attention to what happens inside classrooms—the particulars of teaching and learning—especially in low-income neighborhoods. The news here has been discouraging for quite some time, but, in a painfully ironic twist, things seem to be getting worse as a direct result of the "reform" strategies pursued by the Bush administration, then intensified under President Obama, and cheered by corporate executives and journalists.

In an article published in *Phi Delta Kappan* back in 1991, the late Martin Haberman, a professor at the University of Wisconsin, coined the phrase "pedagogy of poverty." Based on his observations in thousands of urban classrooms, Haberman described a tightly controlled routine in which teachers dispense, and then test students on, factual information; assign seatwork; and punish noncompliance. It is a regimen, he said, "in which learners can 'succeed' without becoming either involved or thoughtful"— and it is noticeably different from the questioning, discovering, arguing,

"Poor Teaching for Poor Children . . . in the Name of Reform" was originally published in Education Week *on April 27, 2011. This is an expanded version of the published article.*

and collaborating that is more common (though by no means universal) among students in suburban and private schools.

Two decades later, Haberman reported that "the overly directive, mind-numbing . . . anti-intellectual acts" that pass for teaching in most urban schools "not only remain the coin of the realm but have become the gold standard." It's how you're *supposed* to teach kids of color.

Natalie Hopkinson, an African American writer, put it this way in a 2011 article called "The McEducation of the Negro": "In the name of reform . . . education—for those 'failing' urban kids, anyway—is about learning the rules and following directions. Not critical thinking. Not creativity. It's about how to correctly eliminate three out of four bubbles."

Those who demand that we "close the achievement gap" generally focus only on results, which in practice refers only to test scores. High-quality instruction is defined as whatever raises those scores. But when teaching strategies *are* considered, there is wide agreement (again, among noneducators) about what constitutes appropriate instruction in the inner city.

The curriculum consists of a series of separate skills, with more worksheets than real books, more rote practice than exploration of ideas, more memorization (sometimes assisted with chanting and clapping) than thinking. In books like *The Shame of the Nation*, Jonathan Kozol, another frequent visitor to urban schools, describes a mechanical, precisely paced process for drilling black and Latino children in "obsessively enumerated particles of amputated skill associated with upcoming state exams."

Not only is the teaching scripted, with students required to answer fact-based questions on command, but a system of almost militaristic behavior control is common, with public humiliation for noncompliance and an array of rewards for obedience that calls to mind the token economy programs developed in prisons and psychiatric hospitals.

Deborah Meier, the educator and author who has founded extraordinary schools in New York and Boston, points out that the very idea of "school" has radically different meanings for middle-class kids, who are "expected to have opinions," and poor kids, who are expected to do what they're told. Schools for the well-off are about inquiry and choices; schools for the poor are about drills and compliance. The two types of institutions "barely have any connection to each other," she says.

Adds Kozol: "The children of the suburbs learn to think and to interrogate reality," while inner-city kids "are trained for nonreflective acquiescence." (Work hard, be nice.) At one of the urban schools he visited, a teacher told him, "If there were middle-class white children here, the parents would rebel at this curriculum and stop it cold."

Among the research that has confirmed the disparity are two studies based on data from the periodic National Assessment of Educational Progress. One found that black children are much more likely than white children to be taught with workbooks or worksheets on a daily basis. The other revealed a racial disparity in how computers are used for instruction, with African Americans mostly getting drill and practice exercises (which, the study also found, are associated with poorer results).

Yet another study, by a researcher at Michigan State University, discovered that students in more affluent neighborhoods were given more choice in their reading, more opportunities to talk with one another about books, the chance to analyze and write poetry and to learn skills in the context of real literature.

Well before his brief tenure as New Jersey's Commissioner of Education, Bret Schundler expressed considerable enthusiasm about the sort of teaching that involves constant drill and repetition and "doesn't allow children not to answer." This approach is "bringing a lot of value-added for our children," he enthused. *Our* children? Does that mean he would send his own kids to that kind of school? Of course not. "Those schools are best for certain children," he explained.

The result is that "certain children" are left farther and farther behind. The rich get richer, while the poor get worksheets.

To be sure, the gap has more to do with socioeconomic factors than with how kids are taught. But to whatever extent education does matter, the pedagogy of poverty traps those who are subject to it. The problem isn't that their education lacks "rigor"—in fact, a single-minded focus on "raising the bar" has served mostly to push more low-income youths out of school—but that it lacks depth and relevance and the capacity to engage students.

Essentially the same point has been made by one educational expert after another, including two prominent African Americans in the field: Linda Darling-Hammond (who observed that the "most counterproductive [teaching] approaches" are "enforced most rigidly in the schools serving the most disadvantaged students") and Claude Steele ("a skills-focused, remedial education . . . virtually guarantee[s] the persistence of the race gap").

Rather than viewing the pedagogy of poverty as a disgrace, however, many of the charter schools championed by the new reformers have concentrated on perfecting and intensifying techniques to keep children "on task" and compel them to follow directions. (Interestingly, their carrot-and-stick methods mirror those used by policy makers to control educators.) Bunches of eager, mostly white, college students are invited to drop by for a couple of years to lend their energy to this dubious enterprise.

Is racism to blame here—or perhaps behaviorism? Or could it be that, at its core, the corporate version of "school reform" was never intended to promote thinking—let alone interest in learning—but merely to improve test results? That pressure is highest in the inner cities, where the scores are lowest. And the pedagogy of poverty can sometimes "work" to raise those scores, which makes everyone happy and inclined to reward those teachers.

Unfortunately, that result is often at the expense of real learning, the sort that more privileged students enjoy, because the tests measure what matters least. Thus, it's possible for the accountability movement to *simultaneously narrow the test-score gap and widen the learning gap*.

What's to be done? In the short run, Deborah Meier is probably right when she remarks, "Only secretly rebellious teachers have ever done right by our least advantaged kids." To do right by them in the open, we would need structural changes that make the best kind of teaching available to the kids who need it most.

And we know it *can* work—which is to say, the pedagogy of poverty is not what's best for the poor. There's plenty of precedent. A three-year study (published by the U.S. Department of Education) of 140 elementary classrooms with high concentrations of poor children found that students whose teachers emphasized "meaning and understanding" were far more successful than those who received basic-skills instruction. The researchers concluded by decisively rejecting "schooling for the children of poverty . . . [that] emphasizes basic skills, sequential curricula, and tight control of instruction by the teacher" (http://files.eric.ed.gov/fulltext/ED353355.pdf).

Remarkable results with low-income students of all ages have also been found with the Reggio Emilia model of early-childhood education, the "performance assessment" high schools in New York, and "Big Picture" schools around the country. All of these start with students' interests and questions; learning is organized around real-life problems and projects. Exploration is both active and interactive, reflecting the simple truth that kids learn how to make good decisions by making decisions, not by following directions. Finally, success is judged by authentic indicators of thinking and motivation, not by multiple-choice tests.

That last point is critical. As long as standardized exams remain our primary way of evaluating, we may never see *real* school reform — only an intensification of traditional practices, with the very worst reserved for the disadvantaged.

A British educator named David Gribble was once speaking in favor of the kind of education that honors children's interests and helps them to think deeply about questions that matter. Of course, he added, that sort of education is appropriate for affluent children. For disadvantaged children, on the other hand, it is . . . *essential*.

PART 4

What Kids Don't Need

CHAPTER 17

Grit
A Skeptical Look at the Latest Educational Fad

A new idea is hatched; it begins to spread; it catches on; it inspires a flurry of books and articles, conferences and seminars. And then it fades away. In the last couple of decades, this cycle has played out many times in our field. Yet no matter how many iterations we witness, it can be hard to recognize that the pattern applies to whatever idea is currently stirring up excitement—or to understand the limits of that idea.

Consider the current buzz about self-regulation: teaching students to exercise self-discipline and self-control, to defer gratification and acquire "grit." To discipline children is to compel them to do what we want. But because we can't always be there to hand out rewards or punishments as their behavior merits, some dream of figuring out a way to equip each child with a "built-in supervisor" (as two social scientists once put it) so he or she will follow the rules and keep working even when we're not around. The most expedient arrangement for us, the people with the power, is to get children to discipline themselves—in other words, to be *self-disciplined*.

Proponents of this idea like to point out that cognitive ability isn't the only factor that determines how children will fare in school and in life. That recognition got a boost with science writer Dan Goleman's book *Emotional*

"Grit: A Skeptical Look at the Latest Educational Fad" was originally published in Independent School *in Fall 2014. The article was adapted from* The Myth of the Spoiled Child: Challenging the Conventional Wisdom About Children and Parenting *(Da Capo Press, 2014), which contains the references to research cited here.*

Intelligence in 1996, which discussed the importance of self-awareness, altruism, personal motivation, empathy, and the ability to love and be loved. But a funny thing has happened to the message since then. When you hear about the limits of IQ these days, it's usually in the context of a conservative narrative that emphasizes not altruism or empathy but a recycled version of the Protestant work ethic. The goal is to make sure kids will resist temptation, override their unconstructive impulses, put off doing what they enjoy in order to grind through whatever they've been told to do—and keep at it for as long as it takes.

Emblematic of this shift is Paul Tough's 2012 book *How Children Succeed*, which opens with a declaration that what matters most for children are qualities like "persistence, self-control, curiosity, conscientiousness, grit, and self-confidence." But that's the last time the reader hears about curiosity or self-confidence. Neither of those words even appears in his index. By contrast, there are lengthy entries for "self-control" and "grit," which occupy Tough for much of the book.

"Grit"—the sort of self-discipline that's required to make people persist at something over a long period of time—was popularized by Angela Duckworth, a University of Pennsylvania researcher, and the idea has met with mostly uncritical acclaim in our field. In fact, it's treated as a fresh insight even though basically the same message has been drummed into us by Aesop's fables, Benjamin Franklin's aphorisms, and Christian denunciations of sloth.

Make no mistake: Duckworth is *selling* grit, not dispassionately investigating its effects. "As educators and parents," she and her colleagues wrote in her very first paper on the topic, "we should encourage children to work not only with intensity but also with stamina." She acknowledges that "grittier individuals, by staying the course, may sometimes miss out on new opportunities." But she doesn't see this as a problem. In fact, grit *means* doing "a particular thing in life and choos[ing] to give up a lot of other things in order to do it." For example, she has no use for children who experiment with several musical instruments. "The kid who sticks with one instrument is demonstrating grit," she says. "Maybe it's more fun to try something new, but high levels of achievement require a certain single-mindedness."

This is our first clue that Duckworth's recommendations emerge not from evidence but from her personal belief that people should spend their time trying to improve at one thing rather than exploring, and becoming reasonably competent at, several things. If you happen to favor breadth and variety, Duckworth offers no reason why you should accept her preference for a life of specialization—or for the idea of grit, which is rooted in that preference.

And I think there are several other reasons why the idea merits our skepticism. First, while we're encouraged to see grit, per se, as desirable, not everything is *worth* doing, let alone doing for extended periods. The amorality of the concept enables the immorality of some individuals who exemplify it. This would be a better world if people who were up to no good had *less* grit. To that extent, persistence is really just one of many attributes that can be useful for reaching a (good or bad) outcome, so it's the choice of goal that ought to come first and count more.

Second, as with self-control more generally, grit can sometimes be inappropriate and unhealthy—even if the activity *isn't* morally objectionable. I'm not denying that it sometimes pays to stick with something over the long haul; few of us want to see our students throw in the towel at the first sign of difficulty. But there are many occasions on which it doesn't make sense to persist with a problem that resists solution, to continue at a task that no longer provides satisfaction. When people *do* keep going under these conditions, they may be displaying a refusal to disengage that's both counterproductive (in terms of outcome) and pathological (in terms of motivation).

Anyone who talks about grit as an unalloyed good may need to be reminded of the proverbial Law of Holes: When you're in one, stop digging. Gritty people sometimes exhibit "nonproductive persistence"; they try, try again even though the result may be either unremitting failure or "a costly or inefficient success that could have been easily surpassed by alternative courses of action," as one group of psychologists explained. And the benefits of knowing when *not* to persist extend to the effects on the individual. Following a year-long study of adolescents, Canadian researchers Gregory Miller and Carsten Wrosch concluded that those "who can disengage from unattainable goals enjoy better well-being . . . and experience fewer symptoms of everyday illness."

Just as the *effects* of displaying unqualified grit may not always be optimal, the *motives* for doing so raise important psychological questions. A theorist who is focused only on measurable behaviors won't bother to ask whether a student who persists does so because she loves what she's doing or because of a desperate (and anxiety-provoking) need to prove her competence. As long as she doesn't give up, we're supposed to nod our approval.

(Interestingly, people who are passionate about what they're doing tend to need a lot less self-discipline to stick with it.)

To know when to pull the plug requires the capacity to adopt a long-term perspective as well as a measure of gumption. Because continuing to do what one has been doing often represents the path of least resistance, it can take guts to cut one's losses and say ¡Basta! And that's as important a message to teach our students as the usefulness of perseverance. Or, to put it differently, what counts is the capacity to *decide* whether and when to persevere — or to exercise self-control, which can also be maladaptive in some circumstances.[1] That's very different from the message that perseverance or self-regulation is valuable in itself.

The main rationale for teaching children to be gritty is to promote academic achievement. That sounds like a worthy goal, but take a moment to reflect on other possible goals one might have — for example, helping them to lead a life that's happy and fulfilling, morally admirable, creative, or characterized by psychological health. Any of those objectives would almost certainly lead to prescriptions quite different from "Do one thing and keep at it."

Moreover, if you look closely at Duckworth's research, the benefits she claims to have demonstrated turn out to be either circular or simply dubious. In one of her studies, she found that freshman cadets at West Point who scored high on her grit questionnaire ("I finish whatever I begin") were less likely to quit during the grueling summer training program. But what does that prove, other than that people who are persistent persist?

Another pair of studies looked at an elite group of middle schoolers who qualified for the National Spelling Bee. Duckworth reported that they performed better in that competition if they were higher in grit, "whereas spellers higher in openness to experience — defined as preferring using their imagination, playing with ideas, and otherwise enjoying a complex mental life — perform[ed] worse." She also found that the most effective preparation strategy was "solitary deliberate practice activities" rather than, say, reading books.

What's striking here aren't the findings themselves but the lesson Duckworth seems to derive from them. If enjoying a complex mental life (or reading for pleasure) interferes with performance in a one-shot contest to see who can spell more obscure words correctly — and if sufficient grittiness to spend time alone memorizing lists of words helps to achieve that goal — this is regarded as an argument in favor of grit. Presumably it also argues against having a complex mental life or engaging in "leisure reading."

(Ironically, even if we were interested in how well kids can spell—by which I mean (a) most kids, not just champion spellers, and (b) as judged by their actual writing rather than in the contrived format of a spelling bee—other research has found that reading, apart from its other benefits, is actually more effective than drill and practice. But to at least some proponents of grit, reading is less onerous, demands less self-discipline, and is therefore less admirable.)

The relevant issue again has more to do with ends than means. How important is it that kids who are exceptionally good spellers win more championships? Should we favor any strategy or personality feature that contributes to that objective—or to anything that could be described as "higher achievement"—regardless of what it involves and what it displaces?

Duckworth is particularly interested to show that self-discipline and grit produce better grades. Her very first experiment found that teachers gave more As to students who tended to put off doing what they enjoy until they finished their homework. But suppose the students with the best grades were those who nodded and smiled at everything their teacher said. Would that argue for encouraging kids to become more obsequious? Or what if self-discipline on the part of adults was associated with more positive evaluations from their supervisors at work? We'd have to conclude that employees who did what their bosses wanted, regardless of whether it was satisfying or sensible, elicited a favorable verdict from those same bosses. But so what?

Good grades, in other words, are often just a sign of approval by the person with the power in a classroom. And even when they serve other functions, grades suffer from low levels of validity and reliability. Moreover, students who pursue higher grades tend to be less interested in what they're learning, more likely to think in a superficial fashion (and less likely to retain information), and inclined to prefer the easiest possible task whenever they have a choice—because the goal isn't to explore ideas but to do whatever is necessary to snag the A. Those who snag a lot of them seem, on average, to be overly conformist and not particularly creative.[2] So if students who are more self-disciplined or persistent get higher grades, that doesn't make a case for grit so much as it points up the limitations of grades as an outcome measure.

_____

Social psychologists sometimes use the term "fundamental attribution error" to describe a tendency to pay so much attention to character, personality, and individual responsibility that we overlook how profoundly the social environment affects what we do and who we are. This error has political implications: The more we focus on people's persistence (or self-discipline more generally), the less likely we'll be to question larger policies and institutions. Consider Paul Tough's declaration that "there is no antipoverty tool we can provide for disadvantaged young people that will be more valuable than the character strengths . . . [such as] conscientiousness, grit, resilience, perseverance, and optimism." Whose interests are served by the astonishing position that "no antipoverty tool"—presumably including Medicaid and public housing—is more valuable than an effort to train poor kids to persist at whatever they've been told to do?

The eagerness among educators to embrace concepts like grit and self-regulation can also be understood as an example of the fundamental attribution error. Driving the study of student performance conducted by Duckworth and her mentor Martin Seligman, for example, was their belief that underachievement *isn't* explained by structural factors—social, economic, or even educational. Rather, they insisted it should be attributed to the students themselves and their "failure to exercise self-discipline." *The entire conceptual edifice of grit is constructed on that individualistic premise*, one that remains popular for ideological reasons even though it's been repeatedly debunked by research.

The most impressive educational activists are those who struggle to replace a system geared to memorizing facts and taking tests with one dedicated to exploring ideas. They're committed to a collaborative approach to schooling that learners will find more engaging. By contrast, those enamored of grit look at the same status quo and ask: How can we get kids to put up with it?

Duckworth has insisted that grit allows people to meet their own goals, but the focus of her research, particularly with children, is on compliance: how to make students pay "attention to a teacher rather than daydreaming," persist "on long-term assignments despite boredom and frustration," choose "homework over TV," and "behav[e] properly in class." In her recent research, she created a task that's deliberately boring, the point being to devise strategies so students will resist the temptation to do something more interesting instead.

This is the mindset that underlies the campaign for grit and self-discipline, even if it isn't always spelled out. Which is why it's critical that those of us who don't share Duckworth's values—and are committed to changing the system rather than just making kids adapt to it—maintain a healthy skepticism about that campaign. While we're at it, we might bring that same skepticism to bear when the next bandwagon rolls through town.

NOTES

1. For more on how self-control can be problematic, see chapter 7 of my book *The Myth of the Spoiled Child* (Da Capo Press, 2014) or the article "Why Self-Discipline Is Overrated," *Phi Delta Kappan*, November 2008: 168–76—available at www.alfiekohn.org/article/self-discipline-overrated.

2. For evidence, we need look no further than research Duckworth herself cites to prove that self-discipline predicts academic performance. One such study found that such performance "seemed as much a function of attention to details and the rules of the academic game as it was of intellectual talent." High-achieving students "were not particularly interested in ideas or in cultural or aesthetic pursuits. Moreover, they were not particularly tolerant or empathic; however, they did seem stable, pragmatic, and task-oriented, and lived in harmony with the rules and conventions of society. Finally, relative to students in general, these superior achievers seemed somewhat stodgy and unoriginal."

CHAPTER 18

What Waiting for a Second Marshmallow *Doesn't* Prove

Traditional schooling isn't working for an awful lot of students. We can respond to that fact either by trying to fix the system (so it meets kids' needs better) or by trying to fix the kids (so they're more compliant and successful at whatever they're told to do). The current enthusiasm for teaching self-discipline and persistence represents a vote for the second option. And underlying self-discipline is the idea of deferring gratification — for example, by putting off doing what you enjoy until you finish your "work." The appeal to many educators of transforming kids from lazy grasshoppers to hard-working ants explains the fresh wave of interest in a series of experiments conducted back in the 1960s known as the marshmallow studies.

By now you've probably heard the summary: At the Stanford University laboratory of a psychologist named Walter Mischel, preschool-age children were left alone in a room after having been told they could get a small treat (a marshmallow or pretzel) by ringing a bell at any time to summon the experimenter. But if they held out until he returned on his own, they could have a bigger treat (two marshmallows or pretzels). The outcome, as it's usually represented, is that the children who were able to wait for an extra treat scored better on measures of cognitive and social skills many years later and had higher SAT scores. Thus, if we teach kids to put off the payoff as long as possible, they'll be more successful.

"What Waiting for a Second Marshmallow Doesn't Prove" was originally published in Education Week *on September 10, 2014. The article was adapted from* The Myth of the Spoiled Child: Challenging the Conventional Wisdom About Children and Parenting *(Da Capo Press, 2014), which contains the references to research cited here.*

But in several ways that simplistic conclusion misrepresents what the research actually found.

1. What mostly interested Mischel wasn't *whether* children could wait for a bigger treat — which, by the way, most of them could. It wasn't even whether waiters fared better in life than non-waiters. Rather, the central question was *how* children go about trying to wait and which strategies help. It turned out that kids waited longer when they were distracted by a toy. What worked best wasn't (in his words) "self-denial and grim determination" but doing something enjoyable while waiting *so that self-control wasn't needed at all.*

Mischel and his colleagues systematically varied the details of the situation to see if this affected children's willingness to wait. These changes included telling them about (vs. showing them) the marshmallow, encouraging them to think about its shape (vs. its taste), and suggesting a distraction strategy (vs. having kids come up with their own). Sure enough, such factors were more important for predicting the outcome than any trait the child possessed. This, of course, is precisely the opposite of the usual message that (a) self-control is a matter of individual character, which (b) we ought to help children develop.

2. Even to the extent that Mischel looked at characteristics of individual children in addition to situational details, when those children were tracked down ten years later, those who had been more likely to wait didn't have any more self-control or willpower than the others.

This makes sense because Mischel's primary focus was on strategies for how to think about (or stop thinking about) something attractive — and how those strategies may be related to other skills down the line. Those later outcomes weren't associated with the ability to defer gratification, per se, but only with the ability to distract oneself when distractions weren't provided by the experimenters. What's more, the ability to invent a distraction turned out to be correlated with plain old intelligence — a very interesting finding because other writers (like Duckworth) have argued that intelligence and self-discipline are totally different things and that we should train children to acquire the latter.

It shouldn't be surprising that kids' capacity to figure out a way to think about something other than the food was associated with their SAT scores. It's not that willpower makes kids successful; it's that the same loose cluster of mental proficiencies that helped them with distraction when they were young also helped them score well on a test of reasoning when they were older. (In fact, when the researchers held those scores constant, most of the *other* long-term benefits associated with their marshmallow-related behavior disappeared.)

3. Almost everyone who cites these experiments assumes that it's better to wait for two marshmallows — that is, to defer gratification. But is that always true? Mischel, for one, didn't think so. "In a given situation," he and his colleagues wrote, "postponing gratification may or may not be a wise or adaptive choice." Sometimes a marshmallow in the hand is better than two in the bush. It's true, for example, that if you spend too much of your money when you're young, you may regret it when you're old. But how much should you deprive yourself — and perhaps your children — in order to accumulate savings for retirement?

Moreover, while some tasks favor waiting, others favor taking what you can right now. In one experiment, researchers fiddled with the algorithm that determined how points were earned in a simulation game and then tracked the interaction between that change and the players' personalities. "Impulsivity," they concluded, "is not a purely maladaptive trait but one whose consequences hinge on the structure of the decision-making environment."

And here's another twist: The inclination to wait depends on one's experiences. "For a child accustomed to stolen possessions and broken promises, the only guaranteed treats are the ones you have already swallowed," remarked a group of social scientists at the University of Rochester. In 2013 they conducted an experiment in which children were encouraged to wait for "a brand-new set of exciting art supplies" rather than using the well-worn crayons and dinky little stickers that were already available. After a few minutes, the adult returned. Half the kids received the promised, far superior materials. But the other half got only an apology: "I'm sorry, but I made a mistake. We don't have any other art supplies after all."

Then it was time for the marshmallow challenge. And how long did the children wait for two to appear before they gave up and ate the one sitting in front of them? Well, it depended on what had happened earlier. Those for whom the adult had proved unreliable (by failing to deliver the promised art supplies) waited only about three minutes. But those who had learned that good things do come to those who wait were willing to hold off, on average, for a remarkable twelve minutes.

Thus, the decision about whether to defer gratification may tell us what the child has already learned about whether waiting is likely to be worth it. If her experience is that it isn't, then taking whatever is available at the moment is a perfectly reasonable choice. Notice that this finding also challenges the conclusion that the capacity to defer gratification produces various later-life benefits. Self-restraint can be seen as a result of earlier experiences, not an explanation for how well one fares later.

The Rochester study clarifies what may have been going on in Mischel's original experiments, where there was no effort to learn about the children's lives before they walked into his lab. But even on its own Mischel's work doesn't support the case for willpower and self-denial that traditionalists have tried to make. Waiting for a bigger treat doesn't always make sense. And even when it does, the question is What changes in the environment can facilitate that choice such that self-discipline becomes less important?

Perhaps the broader message for educators is this: Focus less on "fixing the kids" and more on improving what and how they're taught.

CHAPTER 19

What Do Kids Really Learn from Failure?

Closely connected to demands to teach children to show more persistence and perseverance is the proposition that children benefit from plenty of bracing experiences with frustration and failure. Ostensibly this will motivate them to try even harder next time and prepare them for the rigors of the unforgiving Real World. However, it's also said that children don't get enough of these experiences because they're overprotected by well-meaning but clueless adults who hover too close and catch them every time they stumble.

This basic story, which has found favor with journalists as well as certain theorists and therapists, seems plausible on its face because some degree of failure *is* unavoidable and we obviously want our kids to be able to deal with it. On closer inspection, though, I think there are serious problems with both the descriptive and prescriptive claims we're being asked to accept.

Is failure rare? The idea that "kids today" have it too easy is part of a broader conservative worldview that's been around for a long, long time. Children are routinely described as coddled and indulged, overprotected and overpraised. But I've been unable to find any data to support this claim, which may explain why it rests mostly on provocative anecdotes. Even if we could agree on how much protection (or parenting) merits the prefix *over-*, there's simply no proof that the phenomenon is widespread, much less that it's more common today than it was ten, twenty, fifty, or one hundred years ago.

"What Do Kids Really Learn from Failure?" was originally published as a blog post on October 3, 2012.

Moreover, even if it were shown that some parents cushion their children more than you or I think they should, that doesn't mean these kids are unacquainted with frustration or failure. To see life through a child's eyes for even a short time is to realize that, quite apart from a parent's willingness to intervene, children frequently come up short, don't get what they want, and find themselves on the receiving end of critical judgments from their peers or adults.

Is failure useful? A hypothetical child who managed to succeed in every one of his endeavors, or who always got everything he desired, might well find it hard to cope if things suddenly turned sour. But are we entitled to conclude from this fanciful thought experiment that failure is beneficial, or that parents and teachers should deliberately stand back rather than help out?

Research certainly doesn't support the idea that failure or disappointment is constructive in itself. Children are not best prepared for unpleasant experiences that may come later by being exposed to a lot of unpleasantness while they're young. We may *want* kids to rebound from failure, but that doesn't mean it's usually going to happen — or that the experience of failure makes that desired outcome more likely.

In fact, studies find that when kids fail, they tend to construct an image of themselves as incompetent and even helpless, which leads to more failure. (They also come to prefer easier tasks and lose interest in whatever they're doing.) In one study, students were asked to solve problems that were rigged to ensure failure. Then they were asked to solve problems that were clearly within their capabilities. What happened? Even the latter problems paralyzed them because a spiral of failure had been set into motion. By the same token, if an adult declines to step in and help when kids are frustrated, that doesn't make them more self-sufficient or self-confident: It mostly leaves them feeling less supported, less secure about their own worthiness, and more doubtful about the extent to which the parent or teacher really cares about them.

Have some people experienced failure but then gone on to be wildly successful? Obviously. But things don't work out this way for most people. And even when it does happen, we can't conclude that experience with failure was responsible for the success. (Also, we should be careful to define what we mean by "successful." One can end up rich or famous without being an admirable or psychologically healthy human being.)

What determines the impact of failure? Why do some people throw in the towel as soon as things get tough? Why do other people get back on the horse? (And why are so many of us unable to discuss these issues without re-sorting to stale metaphors?) To talk about grit and resilience is to focus on the attributes of individuals. But it may make more sense to look at the situations in which people find themselves and the nature of the tasks they're being asked to do.

Challenge—which carries with it a risk of failure—is a part of learning. That's not something we'd want to eliminate. But when students who are tripped up by challenges respond by tuning out, acting out, or dropping out, they sometimes do so not because of a deficiency in their makeup (lack of stick-to-itiveness) but because those challenges—what they were asked to do—aren't particularly engaging or relevant. Finger-wagging adults who ex-hort students to "do their best" sometimes don't offer a persuasive reason for why a given task should be done at all, let alone well. And if the rejoinder is that it doesn't matter if the assignment is just busywork because kids need to develop "good work habits" across the board, well, a reasonable person would wonder who stands to benefit when children are taught to work hard at any-thing that they're assigned to do by someone with more power.

A second explanation for students' not rebounding after they fail at what they were asked to do is that they weren't really "asked" to do it—they were *told* to do it: deprived of any say about the content or context of the cur-riculum. People of all ages are more likely to persevere when they have a chance to make decisions about things that affect them. Thus, the absence of choice might be a better explanation than a character defect for giving up.

And here's yet another possibility. Maybe the problem is that the educa-tional environment emphasizes *how well* students are doing rather than *what* they're doing: It's all about achievement! performance! results! rigor! and not about the learning itself. Educational psychologists have found that when students are induced to think about grades and test scores—particularly, though not exclusively, when the point is to do better than everyone else—they will naturally attempt to avoid unnecessary risks. If the goal is to get an A, then it's rational to pick the easiest possible task. Giving up altogether just takes this response to its logical conclusion. "I'm no good at this, so why bother?" is not unreasonable when school is primarily about establishing how good you are.

Jerome Bruner said this: We want students to "experience success and failure not as reward and punishment but as information." That's a mar-velous way to think about reframing unsuccessful experiences: My experi-ment, or my essay, didn't turn out the way I had hoped, and the reason that happened offers valuable clues for how I might take a different approach tomorrow. But this requires us (the adults) to do more than reframe or encourage. We have to address the structural factors that get in the way. For example, a student isn't going to view letter or number grades as informational feedback; they'll be seen as rewards and punishments, in part because that's exactly what they're intended to be.

The problem isn't with kids' attitudes or motivation as much as it is with our practices and policies. Yet potential problems with the latter are typically ignored by people who tell kids to grit their teeth, pull up their socks, and keep trying. Worse, these people may explicitly *endorse* such problematic practices or even call for more rigorous or competitive grading and testing. Some researchers use them to define success and failure — with high grades or test scores uncritically accepted as a positive outcome for measuring the effects of grit or perseverance.

Indeed, many people oppose even mild attempts to make the whole grading experience less debilitating, such as eliminating zeroes for individual assignments (given that zeroes, when averaged in with other marks, can drag down a child's overall grade disproportionately). Not long ago, a Canadian teacher became a conservative folk hero for defying his district's no-zero policy. He insisted on his prerogative to punish students by giving them the lowest possible grade.

Those who came to his defense invoked the familiar rhetoric of accountability, high standards, and the need to prepare kids for the real world. But ponder the irony! Many students whom a teacher brands with zeroes already see themselves as failures. They're likely to experience his insistence that they be "held accountable" as yet another dose of humiliation and punishment. (And it's the students' perception, not the teacher's intention, that determines the result.) The idea that another goose egg will snap them out of their cycle of failure and put them on the road to success is, to put it gently, naïve.[1]

In short, there's reason to doubt the popular claim that kids have too little experience with failure. Or that more such experience would be good for them. What is clear is that the very environments that play up the importance of doing well make it even less likely that doing poorly will have any beneficial effect.

NOTE

1. On the other hand, some people's get-tough response is actually more moralistic than practical. The point may not have been to produce a better outcome for students at all but to make sure they don't "get away with" something. If you do something bad, something bad must be done to you—regardless of the effect.

CHAPTER 20

Criticizing (Common Criticisms of) Praise

Over the last few years I've had the odd experience of seeing my work cited with approval by people whose views on the issue in question are diametrically opposed to my own. The issue I have in mind is praise. I'm troubled by it, as are the people who quote me, but for very different reasons. So I thought I'd try to set the record straight even if the result is that I antagonize some folks who seem to regard me as an ally.

I explained my concerns about praise — and outlined alternatives to it — in two books (*Punished by Rewards* and *Unconditional Parenting*) and in an article called "Five Reasons to Stop Saying 'Good Job!,'" so I'll quickly summarize my arguments here rather than trying to lay them out in sufficient detail to convince a skeptic.

Praise is a verbal reward, often doled out in an effort to change someone's behavior, typically someone with less power. More to the point, it's likely to be experienced as controlling regardless of the praiser's intention. Praise is a pat on the head, "pat" being short for "patronizing," that's offered when the child (or student or employee) impresses or pleases the parent (or teacher or manager). Like other forms of reward (or punishment), it's a way of "doing to," rather than "working with," people. My value judgment is that the latter is more respectful and therefore preferable to the former.

Value judgments aside, though, praise has very real and unfortunate effects — again, just like other types of rewards — particularly when it's offered

---

"Criticizing (Common Criticisms of) Praise" was originally published as a blog post on February 3, 2012.

to a child by an adult. It tends to reduce the recipient's interest in the task, or commitment to the action, that elicited the praise. Often it also reduces the quality of whatever was done. The effect of a "Good job!" is to devalue the activity itself—reading, drawing, helping—which comes to be seen as a mere means to an end, the end being to receive that expression of approval. If approval isn't forthcoming next time, the desire to read, draw, or help is likely to diminish. My objection here isn't to giving feedback (which is purely informational), as in "Here's what I noticed," but to offering a judgment, as in "I like the way you. . . ." Positive judgments are ultimately no more constructive than negative ones.

Some years after laying out these concerns, I came to realize that praise was troubling in yet another way: It signals conditional acceptance. Children learn that they're valued—and, by implication, valuable—only when they live up to the standards of a powerful other. Attention, acknowledgment, and approval must be *earned* by doing a "job" that someone else decides is "good." Thus, positive reinforcement is not only different from, but antithetical to, the *unconditional* care that children need: to be loved just for who they are, not for what they do. It's no surprise that this strategy was designed to elicit certain behaviors rather than to promote children's psychological health.

That's the basic critique. Now allow me to point out what it isn't.

1. It's not an argument for praising *less frequently*. The problem isn't with how often it's done but with the nature of a verbal reward—how it's intended and especially how it's construed.

2. It's not an argument for offering more *meaningful* praise—as distinguished from the "empty" kind. Quite the opposite, in fact. Yes, some teachers and parents reflexively hand out the equivalent of a doggie biscuit every few minutes, the result being that kids habituate to it and it has no impact. If so, good! It may be a waste of breath, but at least it's not doing too much damage. The kind of praise that's rationed and carefully timed for maximum impact is more manipulative and more harmful.

3. It's not an argument for praising people's *effort* rather than their *ability*. That distinction, which has attracted considerable attention over the last few years, is derived from the work of Carol Dweck. I have been greatly impressed and influenced by Dweck's broader argument, which spells out the negative effects of leading people to attribute success (or failure) to their intelligence (or its absence). Intelligence, like other abilities, is often regarded as innate and fixed: You either got it, or you ain't.

But the critical distinction between effort and ability doesn't map neatly onto the question of praise. First of all, while it's impossible to dispute Dweck's well-substantiated contention that praising kids for being smart is counterproductive, praising them for the effort they've made can also backfire: It may communicate that they're really not very capable and therefore unlikely to succeed at future tasks. (If you're complimenting me just for trying hard, it must be because I'm a loser.) At least three studies have supported exactly this concern.

Second, the more attention we give to the problems of ability-focused praise in particular, the more we're creating the misleading impression that praise in general is harmless or even desirable. Of the various problems I've laid out — its status as an extrinsic inducement and a mechanism of control, its message of conditional acceptance, its detrimental effects on intrinsic motivation and achievement — none is limited to the times when we praise someone's ability. In fact, I'm not convinced that this type is any worse than other praise with respect to these deeper issues.

Third, to the extent that we want to teach the importance of making an effort — the point being that people have some control over their future accomplishments — praise really isn't required at all. (Dweck readily conceded this in a conversation we had some years ago. Indeed, she didn't seem particularly attached to praise as a strategy, and she willingly acknowledged its potential pitfalls.) It would be a useful exercise, for an individual teacher or as a staff development activity, to figure out how we might be leading students to conclude that failing at a task means they just don't have what it takes. What policies, and what approaches to assessment in particular, might incline someone to think that ability, as opposed to effort, makes the difference?

4. Most of all, this is not an argument that praise is objectionable because we're spoiling our kids, *overcelebrating* their accomplishments, and convincing them that they're more talented than they really are. If you have read any article critical of praise in the last two decades, it has probably proceeded from this premise, which represents a form of social conservatism widely shared even by political liberals. Here, praise is seen as just one more symptom of a culture of overindulgence, right alongside grade inflation, helicopter parenting, excessive focus on self-esteem, and the practice of handing out trophies to all the participants.

Microsoft Word lacks a font sufficiently bold to emphasize how starkly this sensibility — and this reason for opposing praise — differs from my own.

In fact, I've been so troubled by the values underlying this critique and its mistaken empirical assumptions (about child development, learning, and the psychology of motivation) that I recently wrote a book on the subject called *The Myth of the Spoiled Child*. You can imagine my reaction, then, when people who think along these lines invoke something I've written about praise to help make their case.

Some of these people wax indignant that children are praised—and consequently come to expect praise—for doing things that they ought to do just because they've been told to do them. This old-school argument for un-questioning (and unrewarded) obedience contrasts sharply with my claim that praise is more likely to function as a tool for imposing our will and elic-iting compliance. Like much of what is called "overparenting," praise doesn't signify permissiveness or excessive encouragement; to the contrary, it is an exercise in (sugar-coated) control. It is an extension of the old-school model of families, schools, and workplaces—yet, remarkably, most of the criti-cisms of praise you're likely to read assume that it's a *departure* from the old school, and that that's a bad thing.

Praise is typically faulted for being given out too readily (see point #2, above), with the bar having been set too low. We're told that kids should do more to deserve each "Good job!" they get—which is a way of saying it should be *more* conditional. Again, this is exactly the opposite of my objec-tion to the conditionality inherent in rewards. The problem isn't that kids ex-pect praise for everything they do. The problem is with our need for control, our penchant for placing conditions on our love, and our continued reliance on the long-discredited premises of behaviorism.

You may not be persuaded by my critical analysis of praise and the as-sumptions that underlie its use. Just don't confuse it with criticisms that reflect an entirely different set of values.

CHAPTER 21

Five Not-So-Obvious Propositions About Play

- Children should have plenty of opportunities to play.

- Even young children have too few such opportunities these days, particularly in school settings.

These two propositions—both of them indisputable and important—have been offered many times.[1] The second one in particular reflects the "cult of rigor" at the center of corporate-style school reform. Its devastating impact can be mapped horizontally (with test preparation displacing more valuable activities at every age level) as well as vertically (with pressures being pushed down to the youngest grades, resulting in developmentally inappropriate instruction). The typical American kindergarten now resembles a really bad first-grade classroom. Even preschool teachers, as I suggested in chapter 15, are told to sacrifice opportunities for imaginative play in favor of drilling young children until they master a defined set of skills.

As with anything that needs to be said—and isn't being heard by the people in power—there's a temptation to keep saying it. But because we've been reminded so often of those two basic contentions about play, I'd like to offer five other propositions on the subject that seem less obvious, or at least less frequently discussed.

"Five Not-So-Obvious Propositions About Play" was originally published as a blog post on November 17, 2011. It was adapted from remarks delivered at the Coalition of Essential Schools Fall Forum in Providence, Rhode Island, on November 12, 2011.

1. "Play" is being sneakily redefined. Whenever an educational concept begins to attract favorable attention, its name will soon be invoked by people (or institutions) even when what they're doing represents a diluted, if not thoroughly distorted, version of the original idea. Much that has been billed as "progressive," "authentic," "balanced," "developmental," "student-centered," "hands on," "differentiated," "personalized," or "discovery based" turns out to be discouragingly traditional. So it is with play: "Most of the activities set up in 'choice time' or 'center time' [in early-childhood classrooms] and described as play by some teachers, are in fact teacher-directed and involve little or no free play, imagination, or creativity," as the Alliance for Childhood's Ed Miller put it.[2] Thus, the frequency with which people still *talk* about play shouldn't lead us to conclude that all is well.

2. Younger and older children ought to have the chance to play together. Peter Gray, a psychologist at Boston College, points out that older kids are uniquely able to provide support—often referred to as "scaffolding"—for younger kids in mixed-age play. The older children may perform this role even better than adults because they're closer in age to the younger kids and also because they don't "see themselves as responsible for the younger children's long-term education [and therefore] typically don't provide more information or boosts than the younger ones need. They don't become boring or condescending."[3]

3. Play isn't just for children. The idea of play is closely related to imagination, inventiveness, and that state of deep absorption that Mihaly Csikszentmihalyi dubbed "flow." Read virtually any account of creativity, in the humanities or the sciences, and you'll find mentions of the relevance of daydreaming, fooling around with possibilities, looking at one thing and seeing another, embracing the joy of pure discovery, asking "What if . . . ?" The argument here isn't just that we need to let little kids play so they'll be creative when they're older, but that play, or something quite close to it, should be part of a teenager's or adult's life, too.[4]

4. The point of play is that it has no point. I didn't know whether to laugh or shudder when I read this sentence in a national magazine—written, as it happens, by Paul Tough: "Kids need careful adult guidance and instruction before they are able to play in a productive way."[5] But I will admit that I, too, sometimes catch myself trying to justify play in terms of its usefulness.

The problem is that to insist on its benefits risks violating the spirit, if not the very meaning, of play. In his classic work on the subject, *Homo Ludens*, the Dutch historian Johan Huizinga described play as "a free activity standing quite consciously outside ordinary life as being 'not serious' but at the same absorbing the player intensely and utterly." One plays because it's fun to do so, not because of any instrumental advantage it may yield. The point isn't to perform well or to master a skill, even though those things might end up happening. In G. K. Chesterton's delightfully subversive aphorism, "If a thing is worth doing at all, it's worth doing badly."

Play, then, is about process, not product. It has no goal other than itself. And among the external goals that are inconsistent with play is a deliberate effort to do something better or faster than someone else. If you're keeping score—in fact, if you're competing at all—then what you're doing isn't play.

Implicit in all of this is something that John Dewey pointed out: "'Play' denotes the psychological attitude of the child, not . . . anything which the child externally does." As is so often the case, focusing on someone's behavior, that which can be seen and measured, tells us very little. It's people's goals (or, in this case, lack of goals), their perspectives, and experiences of the situation that matter. Thus, Dewey continues, "any given or prescribed system" or activities for promoting play should be viewed skeptically lest these be inconsistent with the whole idea.[6]

Such is the context for understanding well-meaning folks (like me) whose lamentations about diminishing opportunities for play tend to include a defensive list of its practical benefits. Play is "children's work"! Play teaches academic skills, advances language development, promotes perspective taking, conflict resolution, the capacity for planning, and so on. To drive the point home, Deborah Meier wryly suggested that we stop using the word *play* altogether and declare that children need time for "self-initiated cognitive activity."

But what if we had reason to doubt some or all of these advantages? What if, as a couple of researchers have indeed suggested, empirical claims about what children derive from play—at least in terms of academic benefits—turned out to be overstated?[7] Would we then conclude that children shouldn't be able to play, or should have less time to do so? Or would we insist that play is intrinsically valuable, that it's not only defined by the absence of external goals for those who do it but that it doesn't need external benefits in order for children to have the *opportunity* to do it? Anyone who endorses that position would want to be very careful about defending play based on its alleged payoffs, just as we'd back off from other bargains with the devil, such as arguing that teaching music to children improves their proficiency at math, or that a given progressive innovation raises test scores.

5. Play isn't the only alternative to "work." I've never been comfortable using the word *work* to describe the process by which children make sense of ideas — which is to say, adopting a metaphor derived from what adults do in factories and offices to earn money.[8] To express this concern, however, isn't tantamount to saying that students should spend all day in school playing. Work and play don't exhaust the available options. There's also *learning*, whose primary purpose is neither play-like enjoyment (although it can be deeply satisfying) nor work-like completion of products (although it can involve intense effort and concentration). It's not necessary to *work* in order to experience challenge or excellence, and it's not necessary to *play* in order to experience pleasure.

But there's still a need for pure play. And that need isn't being met.

NOTES

1. See the work of the Alliance for Childhood (www.allianceforchildhood.org/ playwork), statements by the National Association for the Education of Young Children (www.naeyc.org/play), and such recent books as Deborah Meier et al.'s *Playing for Keeps* (Teacher's College Press, 2010), Dorothy Singer et al.'s *Play = Learning* (Oxford University Press, 2009), Vivian Gussin Paley's *A Child's Work* (University of Chicago Press, 2005), and David Elkind's *The Power of Play* (Da Capo Press, 2007).

2. Miller is quoted in Linda Jacobson, "Children's Lack of Playtime Seen as Troubling Health, School Issue," *Education Week*, December 3, 2008. A few years later, Elizabeth Graue, a professor of early childhood education at the University of Wisconsin, made exactly the same point: "What counts as play in many classrooms are highly controlled centers that focus on particular content labeled as 'choice' but that are really directed at capturing a specific content-based learning experience, such as number bingo or retelling a story exactly as the teacher told it on a flannel board" ("Are We Paving Paradise?," *Educational Leadership*, April 2011: 15).

3. See Gray's article "The Value of Age-Mixed Play," *Education Week*, April 16, 2008: 32, 26.

4. One of many resources on this topic: the National Institute for Play (www.nifplay.org), founded by Dr. Stuart Brown. Also, if you ever have the

opportunity to see Saul Bass' short documentary film *Why Man Creates* (1968), don't miss it.

5. Paul Tough, "Can the Right Kinds of Play Teach Self-Control?" *New York Times Magazine*, September 27, 2009.

6. John Dewey, *The School and Society* (Chicago: University of Chicago Press, 1915/1990), pp. 118–19.

7. For example, see research by Peter K. Smith and Angeline Lillard in Tom Bartlett, "The Case for Play," *The Chronicle of Higher Education*, February 20, 2011. Available at http://chronicle.com/article/The-Case-for-Play/126382/.

8. Alfie Kohn, "Students Don't 'Work' — They Learn," *Education Week*, September 3, 1997. Available at www.alfiekohn.org/article/students-dont-work-learn.

PART 5

Misrepresenting
the Research

CHAPTER 22

Homework
An Unnecessary Evil?

A new study on the academic effects of homework offers not only some intriguing results but also a lesson on how to read a study — and a reminder of the importance of doing just that: reading studies (carefully) rather than relying on summaries by journalists or even by the researchers themselves.

Let's start by reviewing what we know from earlier investigations.[1] First, no research has ever found a benefit to assigning homework (of any kind or in any amount) in elementary school. In fact, there isn't even a positive *correlation* between, on the one hand, having younger children do some homework (vs. none), or more (vs. less), and, on the other hand, any measure of achievement. If we're making twelve-year-olds, much less five-year-olds, do homework, it's either because we're misinformed about what the evidence says or because we think kids ought to have to do homework *despite* what the evidence says.

Second, even at the high school level, the research supporting homework hasn't been particularly persuasive. There does seem to be a correlation between homework and standardized test scores, but (a) it isn't strong, meaning that homework doesn't explain much of the variance in scores, (b) one prominent researcher, Timothy Keith, who did find a solid correlation, returned to the topic a decade later to enter more variables into the equation simultaneously, only to discover that the improved study showed that homework had no effect after all,[2] and (c) at best we're only talking about a correlation — things that go together — without having proved that

---

"Homework: An Unnecessary Evil?" was originally published as a blog post on November 26, 2012.

doing more homework *causes* test scores to go up. (Take ten seconds to see if you can come up with other variables that might be driving both of these things.)

Third, when homework is related to test scores, the connection tends to be strongest—or, actually, least tenuous—with math. If homework turns out to be unnecessary for students to succeed in that subject, it's probably unnecessary everywhere.

Along comes a new study, then, that focuses on the neighborhood where you'd be most likely to find a positive effect if one was there to be found: math and science homework in high school. Like most recent studies, this one by Adam Maltese and his colleagues[3] doesn't provide rich descriptive analyses of what students and teachers are doing. Rather, it offers an aerial view, the kind preferred by economists, relying on two large datasets (from the National Education Longitudinal Study [NELS] and the Education Longitudinal Study [ELS]). Thousands of students are asked one question— How much time do you spend on homework?—and statistical tests are then performed to discover if there's a relationship between that number and how they fared in their classes and on standardized tests.

It's easy to miss one interesting result in this study that appears in a one-sentence aside. When kids in these two similar datasets were asked how much time they spent on math homework each day, those in the NELS study said 37 minutes, whereas those in the ELS study said 60 minutes. There's no good reason for such a striking discrepancy, nor do the authors offer any explanation. They just move right along—even though those estimates raise troubling questions about the whole project and about all homework studies that are based on self-report. Which number is more accurate? Or are both of them way off? There's no way of knowing. And because all the conclusions are tied to that number, all the conclusions may be completely invalid.[4]

But let's pretend that we really do know how much homework students do. Did doing it make any difference? The Maltese et al. study looked at the effect on test scores and on grades. They emphasized the latter, but let's get the former out of the way first.

Was there a correlation between the amount of homework that high school students reported doing and their scores on standardized math and science tests? Yes, and it was statistically significant but "very modest": Even assuming the existence of a causal relationship, which is by no means clear, one or two hours' worth of homework every day buys you two or three points on a test. Is that really worth the frustration, exhaustion, family conflict, loss of time for other activities, and potential diminution of interest in learning? And how meaningful a measure were those tests in the first place, since, as the authors concede, they're timed measures of mostly mechanical skills? (Thus, a headline that reads "Study finds homework boosts achievement" can be translated as "A relentless regimen of after-school drill-and-skill can raise scores a wee bit on tests of rote learning.")

But it was grades, not tests, that Maltese and his colleagues really cared about. They were proud of having looked at transcript data in order to figure out "the exact grade a student received in each class [that he or she] completed" so they could compare that to how much homework the student did. Previous research has looked only at students' overall grade-point averages.

And the result of this fine-tuned investigation? There was no relationship whatsoever between time spent on homework and course grade, and "no substantive difference in grades between students who complete homework and those who do not."

This result clearly caught the researchers off-guard. Frankly, it surprised me, too. When you measure "achievement" in terms of grades, you expect to see a positive result — not because homework is academically beneficial but because the same teacher who gives the assignments evaluates the students who complete them, and the final grade is often based at least partly on whether, and to what extent, students did the homework. Even if homework were a complete waste of time, how could it not be positively related to course grades?

And yet it wasn't. Again. Even in high school. Even in math. The study zeroed in on specific course grades, which represents a methodological improvement, and the moral may be: *The better the research, the less likely one is to find any benefits from homework.* (That's not a surprising proposition for a careful reader of reports in this field. We got a hint of that from Timothy Keith's reanalysis and also from the fact that *longer* homework studies tend to find less of an effect.[5])

Maltese and his colleagues did their best to reframe these results to minimize the stunning implications.[6] Like others in this field, they seem to have approached the topic already convinced that homework is necessary and potentially beneficial, so the only question we should ask is *how* — not whether — to assign it. But if you read the results rather than just the authors' spin on them — which you really need to do with the work of others working in this field as well[7] — you'll find that there's not much to prop up the belief that students must be made to work a second shift after they get home from school. The assumption that teachers are just assigning home-work badly, that we'd start to see meaningful results if only it were improved, is harder and harder to justify with each study that's published.

If experience is any guide, however, many people will respond to these results by repeating platitudes about the importance of practice[8] or by complaining that anyone who doesn't think kids need homework is coddling them and failing to prepare them for the "real world" (read: the pointless tasks they'll be forced to do after they leave school). Those open to evidence, however, have now been presented with yet another finding that fails to find any meaningful benefit even when the study is set up to give homework every benefit of the doubt.

NOTES

1. It's important to remember that some people object to homework for reasons that aren't related to the dispute about whether research might show that homework provides academic benefits. They argue that (a) six hours a day of academics are enough, and kids should have the chance after school to explore other interests and develop in other ways — or be able simply to relax in the same way that most adults like to relax after work; and (b) the decision about what kids do during family time should be made by families, not schools. Let's put these arguments aside for now, even though they ought to be (but rarely are) included in any discussion of the topic.

2. Valerie A. Cool and Timothy Z. Keith, "Testing a Model of School Learning: Direct and Indirect Effects on Academic Achievement," *Contemporary Educational Psychology* 16 (1991): 28–44.

3. Adam V. Maltese, Robert H. Tai, and Xitao Fan, "When Is Homework Worth the Time? Evaluating the Association Between Homework and Achievement in High School Science and Math," *The High School Journal*, October/November 2012: 52–72. Abstract at http://ow.ly/fxhOV.

4. Other research has found little or no correlation between how much homework students report doing and how much homework their parents say they do. When you use the parents' estimates, the correlation between homework and achievement disappears. See Harris Cooper, Jorgianne Civey Robinson, and Erika A. Patall, "Does Homework Improve Academic Achievement? A Synthesis of Research, 1987–2003," *Review of Educational Research* 76 (2006): 1–62.

5. To put it the other way around, studies finding the biggest effect are those that capture less of what goes on in the real world by virtue of being so brief. View a small, unrepresentative slice of a child's life and it may appear that homework

makes a contribution to achievement; keep watching, and that contribution is eventually revealed to be illusory. See data provided — but not interpreted this way — by Cooper, *The Battle over Homework*, 2nd ed. (Thousand Oaks, CA: Corwin, 2001).

6. Even the title of their article reflects this: They ask "When Is Homework Worth the Time?" rather than "*Is* Homework Worth the Time?" This bias might seem a bit surprising in the case of the study's second author, Robert H. Tai. He had contributed earlier to another study whose results similarly ended up raising questions about the value of homework. Students enrolled in college physics courses were surveyed to determine whether any features of their *high school* physics courses were now of use to them. At first a very small relationship was found between the amount of homework that students had had in high school and how well they were currently faring. But once the researchers controlled for other variables, such as the type of classes they had taken, that relationship disappeared, just as it had for Keith (see note 2). The researchers then studied a much larger population of students in college science classes — and found the same thing: Homework simply didn't help. See Philip M. Sadler and Robert H. Tai, "Success in Introductory College Physics: The Role of High School Preparation," *Science Education* 85 (2001): 111–36.

7. See chapter 4 ("'Studies Show . . .' — Or Do They?") of my book *The Homework Myth* (Cambridge, MA: Da Capo, 2006), an adaptation of which appears as "Abusing Research: The Study of Homework and Other Examples," *Phi Delta Kappan*, September 2006.

8. On the alleged value of practice, see *The Homework Myth*, pp. 106–18, available at www.alfiekohn.org/students-really-need-practice-homework.

CHAPTER 23

Do Tests Really Help Students Learn or Was a New Study Misreported?

The relationship between educational policies and educational research is both fascinating and disturbing. Sometimes policy makers, including those who piously invoke the idea of "data-driven" practice, pursue initiatives that they favor regardless of the fact that there is no empirical support for them (e.g., high-stakes testing) or even when the research suggests the policy in question is counterproductive (e.g., forcing struggling students to repeat a grade).

Sometimes insufficient attention is paid to the limits of what a study has actually found, such as when a certain practice is said to have been proved "effective," even though that turns out to mean only that it's associated with higher scores on bad tests.

Sometimes research is cited in ways that are disingenuous because anyone who takes the time to track down those studies finds that they actually offer little or no support for the claims in question. (Elsewhere, I've offered examples of this phenomenon in the context of assertions about the supposed benefits of homework—along with details about some of the other ways in which research is under-, over-, or misused.)[1]

Then there's the question of what happens when the press gets involved. It's no secret that the reporting of research is often, shall we say,

"Do Tests Really Help Students Learn or Was a New Study Misreported?" was originally published as a blog post on January 28, 2011.

disappointing: A single experiment's results may be overstated or a broad conclusion may be vaguely attributed to what "studies show," despite the fact that multiple qualifications are warranted. Possible explanations aren't hard to adduce: tight deadlines, lack of expertise, or a reporter's hunger for more column inches or prominent placement (hint: "The results are mixed at best" isn't a sentence that advances journalistic careers).

Whether ideology may also play a role—a tendency to play up certain results more than others—is hard to prove. But recently I found myself wondering whether the *New York Times* would have prominently featured a study, had there been one, showing that taking tests is basically a waste of time for students. After all, the *Times*, like just about every other mainstream media outlet, has been celebrating test-based "school reform" for some time now and, in its news coverage of education, routinely refers to "achievement," teacher "effectiveness," exemplary school "performance," and positive "results," when all that's really meant is higher scores on standardized tests. The media have a lot invested in the idea that testing students is useful and meaningful.

So we probably shouldn't have been surprised to discover that the *Times* ran a lengthy (thirty-something-inch) story on the second page of its national news section under the headline "Take a Test to Really Learn, Research Suggests." And it should be equally unsurprising that the study on which the story was based didn't really support that conclusion at all.

(I'm picking on the *New York Times* because of its prominence, but many news organizations featured this study and described it in similar terms. Other headlines included: "Taking a Test Helps Learning More Than Studying, Report Shows," "Learning Science Better the Old-Fashioned Way," and "Beyond Rote Learning.")

We should begin by noticing that the study itself, which was published in early 2011 in *Science*, had nothing to do with—and therefore offered not the slightest support for—standardized tests.[2] Moreover, its subjects were undergraduates, so there's no way of knowing whether any of its findings would apply to students in K–12 schools.

The real problem with the news coverage, though, is twofold: On closer inspection there are issues with how both the independent variable ("Take a Test") and the dependent variable ("Really Learn") are described.

What interested the two Purdue University researchers, Jeffrey D. Karpicke and Janell R. Blunt, was the idea that trying to remember something that has been taught can aid learning at least as much as the earlier process of encoding or storing that information. Their study consisted of two experiments in which college students either practiced retrieving information they'd learned or engaged in other forms of studying. The former proved more effective.

The type of retrieval practice used in the study was an exercise in which students recalled "as much of the information as they could on a free recall test." But the *idea* of retrieval practice didn't need to involve testing at all. "The *NY Times* article emphasized 'testing,' which is unfortunate, because that's really irrelevant to our central point," Karpicke told me in an email message. "Students could engage in active retrieval of knowledge in a whole variety of ways that aren't 'testing,' per se." For example (as he explained in a subsequent message), they might put the book aside to see how much of it they can recall, try to answer questions about it, or just talk about the topic with someone.

In other words, the experiments didn't show — and never attempted to show — that taking a test works better than studying. They were really comparing one form of studying to another.

Then there's the question of outcome. When I said a moment ago that the study showed retrieval practice was more "effective," the most appropriate response would have been to ask what that word meant in this particular context: more effective at what?

In the first experiment, students were asked both verbatim questions and inference questions that drew on concepts from the text they had been given. In the second experiment, they either took a short-answer test of the material or were asked to create concept maps of that material from memory.

The researchers seemed impressed that practice retrieving facts worked better than making concept maps (with the text in front of them) at preparing students for a closed-book test even when the test itself involved making concept maps. But the students were tested mostly on their ability to recall the material, so it may not be surprising that recall practice proved more useful.

I would argue that this result says less about how impressive the method was than about how unimpressive the goal was. Karpicke and Blunt weren't investigating whether students could construct meaning, apply or generalize concepts to new domains, solve ill-defined problems, draw novel connections or distinctions, or do anything else that could be called creative or higher-order thinking. Now if testing — or any other form of retrieval practice—were shown to enhance *those* capabilities, that would certainly deserve prominent media attention. But this study showed nothing of the sort. Indeed, I know of no reason to believe that tests have any useful role to play in the promotion of truly meaningful learning.

The main contribution of the articles that were published about this study is to remind us of the importance of reading the actual studies being described. To understand why the description of this one was misleading, try to imagine a newspaper running a more accurate account—one with a headline such as "Practice Recalling Facts Helps Students Recall Facts."

NOTE

1. Alfie Kohn, "Abusing Research," *Phi Delta Kappan*, September 2006, available at www.alfiekohn.org/article/abusing-research.

2. Jeffrey D. Karpicke and Janell R. Blunt, "Retrieval Practice Produces More Learning than Elaborative Studying with Concept Mapping," *Science* 331 (2011): 772–75.

CHAPTER 24

Studies Support Rewards and Traditional Teaching. Or Do They?

It's not unusual to read that a new study has failed to replicate — or has even reversed — the findings of an earlier study. The effect can be disconcerting, particularly when medical research announces that what was supposed to be good for us turns out to be dangerous, or vice versa.

Qualifications and reversals also show up in investigations of education and human behavior, but here an interesting pattern seems to emerge. At first a study seems to validate traditional practices, but then subsequent studies — those that follow subjects for longer periods of time or use more sophisticated outcome measures — call that result into question.

That's not really surprising when you stop to think about it. Traditional practices (with respect to teaching students but also to raising children and managing employees) often consist of what might be called a "doing to" — as opposed to a "working with" — approach, the point being to act on people to achieve a specific goal. These strategies sometimes succeed in producing an effect in the short term. Research — which itself is often limited in duration or design — may certify the effort as successful. But when you watch what happens later on, or you look more carefully at the impact of these interventions, the initial findings have a way of going up in smoke.

We've already seen that this is true with homework (chapter 22), where studies that last longer find a diminished effect on achievement or even none at all. Now let's consider two other traditional practices: using rewards to

---

"Studies Support Rewards and Traditional Teaching. Or Do They?" was originally published as a blog post on March 31, 2011.

change people's behavior, and teaching by means of old-fashioned telling (sometimes known as direct instruction). What happens in each case when you look at short-term results, and what happens when you then extend the length of the study?

1. An ambitious investigation of various types of preschools looked specifically at children from low-income families in Illinois. The two educational approaches that produced the greatest impact on achievement in reading and arithmetic were both highly structured, one of them a behaviorist technique called Direct Instruction (or DISTAR) that emphasizes the use of scripted drill in academic skills and praise for correct responses.

Most studies would have left it at that, and the press doubtless would have published the findings, which suggests that this model is superior to more child-centered preschools. (Take that, you progressives!) Luckily, though, this particular group of researchers had both the funding and the interest to continue tracking the children long after they left preschool. And it turned out that with each year that went by, the advantage of two years of regimented reading-skills instruction evaporated, soon proving equivalent—in terms of effects on test scores—to "an intensive 1-hour reading readiness support program" that had been provided to another group. "This follow-up data lends little support for the introduction of formal reading instruction during the preschool years for children from low-income homes," the researchers wrote.

One difference did show up much later, however: Almost three-quarters of the kids in play-oriented and Montessori preschools ended up graduating from high school, as compared to less than half of the direct-instruction kids, which was about the same rate for those who hadn't attended preschool at all. (Other longitudinal studies of preschool have found similar results: The longer you track the kids, the more likely that a drill-and-skill approach will show no benefits and may even appear to be harmful.)[1]

2. Many people who are concerned with promoting healthy lifestyles assume that it makes sense to offer an incentive for losing weight, quitting smoking, or going to the gym. The only real question on this view is how to manage the details of the reward program. In an experiment published in 2008, people who received either of two types of incentives lost more weight after about four months than did those in the control group. (Unfortunately, there was no non-incentive weight-loss program; subjects got either money or no help at all.) At the seven-month mark, however, the effect melted away even if the pounds didn't. There was no statistically significant weight difference between those in either of the incentive conditions and those who received nothing. This result, by the way, is typical of what just about all studies of weight loss and smoking cessation have found: The longer you look, the less chance that rewards will do any good—and, again, they may actually do harm.[2]

3. Belief in the value of rewards is, if anything, even stronger in the corporate world, where it's widely believed—indeed, taken on faith—that dangling financial incentives in front of employees will cause them to work harder. Conversely, if workers are provided with such an incentive and it's then removed, their productivity would be expected to decline. An unusual occurrence in a manufacturing company provided a real-world opportunity to test this assumption: A new collective bargaining agreement for a group of welders resulted in the sudden elimination of a long-standing incentive plan. The immediate result was that production did indeed drop. But as with the preschool study, this researcher decided to continue tracking the company records—and discovered that, in the absence of rewards, the welders' production soon began to rise and eventually reached a level as high or higher than it had been before.[3]

4. Finally, what happens when a second researcher comes along and does a study that's both longer *and* better than the original? Consider a report published in 2004 that showed third and fourth graders who received "an extreme type of direct instruction [in a science unit] in which the goals, the materials, the examples, the explanations, and the pace of instruction [were] all teacher controlled" did better than their classmates who were allowed to design their own procedures. Frankly, the way they had set up the latter condition wasn't representative of the strategies most experts recommend for promoting discovery and exploration. Nevertheless, the finding may have given pause to progressive educators—at least in the context of elementary school science teaching.

Or, rather, it may have given them pause for three years. That's how much time passed before another study was published that investigated the same issue in the same discipline for kids of the same age. The two differences: The second study looked at the effects six months later instead of only one week later; and the second study used a more sophisticated type of assessment of the students' learning. Sure enough, it turned out that any advantage of direct instruction disappeared over time. And on one of the measures, pure exploration not only proved more impressive than direct instruction but also more impressive than a combination of the two—which suggests that direct instruction can be not merely ineffective but counterproductive.[4]

Despite their diversity, these studies hardly exhaust the universe of research that forces a reevaluation of what came before. Still, any observer willing to connect the dots may end up not only waiting for replications to be performed before accepting any preliminary conclusion—a reasonable posture in general—but more skeptical of studies that seem to support traditional practices in particular.

NOTES

1. Merle B. Karnes, Allan M. Shwedel, and Mark B. Williams, "A Comparison of Five Approaches for Educating Young Children from Low-Income Homes." In *As the Twig Is Bent . . . : Lasting Effects of Preschool Programs*, ed. by the Consortium for Longitudinal Studies (Hillsdale, NJ: Erlbaum, 1983). For a summary of other research on early-childhood education, see www.alfiekohn.org/article/early-childhood-education.

2. Kevin G. Volpp et al., "Financial Incentive-Based Approaches for Weight Loss," *Journal of the American Medical Association 300* (December 10, 2008): 2631–37. For a review of other research on the (lack of long-term) effects of financial incentives on weight loss and smoking cessation, see www.alfiekohn.org/miscellaneous/incentives-health-promotion.

3. Harold F. Rothe, "Output Rates Among Welders: Productivity and Consistency Following Removal of a Financial Incentive System," *Journal of Applied Psychology 54* (1970): 549–51.

4. The original study: David Klahr and Milena Nigam, "The Equivalence of Learning Paths in Early Science Instruction: Effects of Direct Instruction and Discovery Learning," *Psychological Science 15* (2004): 661–67. The newer study: David Dean, Jr. and Deanna Kuhn, "Direct Instruction vs. Discovery: The Long View," *Science Education*, 91 (2007): 384–97.

CHAPTER 25

Lowering the Temperature on Claims of Summer Learning Loss

The idea of summer learning loss — the implication of which is that it's risky to give kids a three-month vacation from school because they'll forget much of what they were taught — has become the media's favorite seasonally specific education topic. And that's not just because they're desperate for something to write about when school's out. It's a story we're all predisposed to embrace because we're already nervous about time off for children. It's widely accepted, for example, that kids need to be doing some homework every night during the school year lest they find themselves gravitating to insufficiently constructive activities.

Experts who study creativity like to talk about doing and resting, painting and stepping back from the canvas, thinking about a problem and taking a break during which a new insight may sneak up when we're not expecting it. (Recreation can mean re-creation.) If, on the other hand, we're enamored of a factory model, then we're going to be more focused on productivity than on imagination — and, theologically speaking, more worried about idle hands being the devil's tools. Busyness becomes an end in its own right. We frown when our kids waste time and feel a little ashamed when we ourselves are guilty of it.

I shouldn't be surprised, therefore, that when I've raised questions about the practice of assigning homework on a regular basis, the most common challenge I've faced isn't related to the putative academic benefits but to

"Lowering the Temperature on Claims of Summer Learning Loss" was originally published as a blog post on July 20, 2012.

the prospect that children will just misspend all that time on Facebook or video games. It's kind of interesting, when you think about it: No teacher ever admits to assigning busywork, but this defense of homework itself has nothing to do with the value of the assignments; the point is just to keep kids busy.

It's predictable, then, that we'd be disinclined to let children chill just because it's hot out. We're primed and ready to respond when someone claims that all the progress students have made during the school year will be lost forever if they're allowed to slack off during the summer. It's a Sisyphean metaphor buried in our DNA: The minute you let up in your efforts to roll that rock toward the summit, well, you know what happens. "*L'école d'été pour tous les enfants!*"

What does the research say? Is there any truth to the summer loss claim? Yes. But it's more limited than is generally acknowledged, and it doesn't point to the solution that's most commonly endorsed.

First of all, whatever kind of loss does occur, at least in reading skills, is directly related to students' socioeconomic status. Low-income children are affected disproportionately—to the point that a good part of what is classified as the achievement gap can be explained, statistically speaking, by class-based differences in what happens over the summer. The "summer shortfall . . . [of] low-SES youth . . . relative to better-off children contributes to the perpetuation of family advantage and disadvantage across generations."[1] That's very different from sweeping claims about learning, per se, being something that's inevitably lost when you take a break.

Second, to the extent that low-income kids are likely to lose ground in reading proficiency, Richard Allington, who specializes in this very issue, points out that summer school (and summer homework assignments) aren't necessary or even sensible. Rather, he and his colleagues have shown that the key is to ensure "easy and continuing access to self-selected books for summer reading"[2]—a solution that's not only a lot cheaper than summer school but a lot less likely to cause kids' *interest* in learning to evaporate in a sweltering classroom.

Third, in evaluating the nature and extent of the problem, it's important to keep in mind that virtually all of the research, like almost all talk about the achievement gap itself, is limited to what shows up on standardized tests. Here's the question we should be asking: "Is there still a summer loss problem when we use more meaningful assessments, or is it an artifact of exams that we already know to be deeply misleading (and to have bias built into them in various ways)?" The answer is: We just don't know. For the time being, then, we should refer to the phenomenon as "summer loss on standardized tests."

Finally, even within standardized test measures, summer loss mostly applies to "factual and procedural knowledge" such as "math computation and spelling skills," according to the 1996 meta-analysis that's still the most widely cited source on the topic.[3] This echoes what we know about the whole idea of "time on task," which turns out to have a much less significant relationship to learning outcomes when those outcomes are intellectually ambitious. More time reliably leads to higher achievement mostly when the task involves very little thinking.

As progressive educators have been pointing out for a long time, one of the flaws of traditional instruction is that it consists of transmitting a bunch of facts and skills to students, which they then promptly forget. Summer loss thus should be seen not as a sad but inescapable truth about education but as one more indictment of *traditional* education, with its reliance on lectures, textbooks, worksheets, grades, tests, and homework—all employed in the service of making students cram bits of knowledge into their short-term memories. (And how absurd to think that the solution to this predictable forgetting is to give students more of the same!)

By the time September rolls around, kids may indeed be unable to recall what they were told in April: the distance between the earth and the moon, or the definition of a predicate, or the approved steps for doing long division. But they're much less likely to forget how to set up an experiment to test their own hypothesis (if they had the chance to *do* science last spring), or how to write sentences that elicit a strong reaction from a reader (if they were invited to play with prose with that goal in mind), or what it *means* to divide one number into another (if they were allowed to burrow into the heart of mathematical principles rather than being turned into carbon-based calculators).

Summer learning loss? It's just a subset of life learning loss—when the learning was dubious to begin with.

NOTES

1. Karl L. Alexander et al., "Lasting Consequences of the Summer Learning Gap," *American Sociological Review* 72 (2007): 175.

2. Richard L. Allington et al., "Addressing Summer Reading Setback Among Economically Disadvantaged Elementary Students," *Reading Psychology* 31 (2010): 423.

3. Harris Cooper et al., "The Effects of Summer Vacation on Achievement Test Scores," *Review of Educational Research* 66 (1996): 260.

CHAPTER 26

Is Parent Involvement in School Really Useful?

When people who write about agriculture or dentistry tackle the important issues in their respective fields, do they try to shake things up? Are they feisty and willing to peer beneath the surface of whatever topic they're exploring? I have no idea. But I do know that those qualities are awfully hard to find in what's written about education.

Consider the question of parent involvement in schooling. Almost everything published on this subject leaves the ideological foundations of the discussion unexamined. Either we're treated to a predictable announcement that Involvement Is Good ("Parents should do more!") or else we're warned that some folks have a tendency to get, well, you know, a little *too* involved. ("Jeremy, I'm wondering whether you might have had some help with your science fair project? I ask only because it's unusual for a sixth grader to build a working nuclear reactor.") Put these two themes together and the message seems to be that the interest parents take in their children's education is either inadequate or excessive.

Does that mean there's a sweet spot in the middle that consists of just enough involvement? Or are we looking at an example of what a statistician might call a bimodal distribution when involvement is plotted against socioeconomic status: Poor parents don't do enough; affluent parents do too much?

"Is Parent Involvement in School Really Useful?" was originally published as a blog post on February 6, 2013.

Let's begin by noticing that the whole question is framed by the extent to which educators think parents ought to be involved. The parents' point of view is typically absent from such discussions. And, of course, no thought is given to the *student's* perspective — what role kids might want their parents to play (or to avoid playing). But then that's true of so many conversations about education that we scarcely notice its absence.

There's something both short-sighted and arrogant about exhorting low-income parents to show up at school events or make sure the homework gets done. The presumption seems to be that these parents lack interest or commitment — as opposed to spare time, institutional savvy, comfort level, or fluency in English. Annette Lareau and other sociologists have described how class differences play out in terms of parental advocacy — including why poorer and less-educated parents may be less effective when they do become involved.[1]

But even observers who are sensitive to issues of class don't always take a step back to ask what kind of involvement we're talking about, and to what ends. As is so often the case, our questions tend to be more quantitative than qualitative, with the result that we focus only on how *much* parents are involved.

Imagine someone who monitors his or her child's schooling very closely, for example, and doesn't hesitate to advocate for — or against — certain policy changes and resource allocation decisions. Is that a good thing? Rather than just asking whether the level or style of advocacy is effective, we'd also want to know whether this parent is asking for changes that will benefit all children or mostly just his or her own child (possibly at the expense of others). Our intensely individualistic, free-market-oriented culture — witness the growing push for charter schools, vouchers, and privatization — encourages us to see education not a public good but as just another commodity one shops for, and to evaluate its effectiveness in terms of how much *my kid* gets out of it. Thus, those of us who value the cause of equity have reason to be disturbed by many sorts of parent involvement — not just because some are more involved, or better at being involved, than others but because of what that involvement is intended to achieve and for whom.[2]

Proponents of progressive education, too, have reason to be disturbed by the focus of much involvement, even in individual classrooms. What are the pushiest parents pushing for? If they're judging schools by test scores and children by grades, if they're demanding more traditional forms of math and reading instruction, tighter regulation of students, and more homework, then the content of their agenda will strike us as more relevant than the degree of their involvement. Some of us may be inclined to ask, "How can we invite these parents to reconsider whether their preferences are really consistent with their long-term objectives for their children?" And: "What would it take to create a powerful parent constituency pushing in the other direction?"

Likewise, while everyone wants parents to be engaged with what their children are doing in school, what matters more is the nature of that engagement. There's a big difference between a parent who's focused on *what* the child is doing—that is, on the learning itself—and a parent who's focused on *how well* the child is doing. To ask "So, honey, what's your theory about why the Civil War started?" or "If you had written that story, would you have left the character wondering what happened, the way the author did?" represents a kind of engagement that promotes critical thinking and enthusiasm about learning. To ask "Why only a B+ [or a 3 on the rubric]?" is a kind of engagement that *undermines* both of these things.[3]

Of course, parents wouldn't be asking the latter questions if the school weren't reducing students to letters and numbers in the first place; they're taking their cue from educators who blur the differences between a focus on learning and a focus on performance, or between intrinsic and extrinsic motivation. Nevertheless, this issue seems to have escaped the notice of just about everyone who writes on the topic of parent involvement.

Finally, there's the matter of whether established educational practices are, on the one hand, accepted uncritically, so that the only question is whether kids are compliant and successful by established criteria, or whether, on the other hand, those practices are examined to see if they make sense. Not surprisingly, it's the rare educator who encourages the latter. The result is that parents are urged to become more involved (*ma non troppo!*) in a way that may be more about perpetuating the status quo than about doing what's in children's best interest.

A "partnership" between school and family sounds lovely unless that partnership is perceived by the child as an alliance against him. If the purpose is to coerce him into obeying rules that may not be reasonable, or to "live up to his potential" by working harder at assignments of dubious value, then we'd want parents to ask penetrating questions about the school's practices. Parents should aim higher than helping teachers to make children toe the line.

Homework offers a vivid example. Even on its own terms, parental involvement may not be beneficial. A recent study of middle schoolers found that "the more teachers intended to establish a close link with parents and to involve them in the homework process, the less positive the student outcomes were."[4] And a review of *fifty* studies found that, while parental involvement in general was "associated with achievement," the one striking exception was parental help with homework, where there was no positive effect.[5]

But the predominant outcome measures in such studies are test scores, which means that even if "positive effects" did turn up, they wouldn't impress those of us who doubt the validity and value of standardized test results. Nor would they tell us about the possible *negative* effects that certain kinds of involvement might have on students' creativity, psychological health, excitement about learning, their relationship with their parents, and so on.

Given the dubious benefits of homework, what kids need are parents willing to question the conventional wisdom and to organize others to challenge school practices when that seems necessary. What kids *don't* need is the kind of parental involvement that consists of pestering them to make sure they do their homework—whether or not it's worth doing.

Exhortations for more "parental involvement" remind me of calls to be "a good citizen": In the abstract, everyone is for it. But inspected closely, what's most often meant by the term turns out to be considerably more complicated and even worthy of skepticism.

NOTES

1. For example, see Lareau's book *Home Advantage: Social Class and Parental Intervention in Elementary Education* (Philadelphia: Falmer, 1989).

2. Alfie Kohn, "Only for *My* Kid: How Privileged Parents Undermine School Reform," *Phi Delta Kappan*, April 1998. Available at www.alfiekohn.org/article/kid.

3. I review research relevant to this distinction in my book *The Schools Our Children Deserve* (Boston: Houghton Mifflin, 1999), chapter 2. Also see this twenty-minute video presentation: http://cfee.me/PSPvidAK.

4. Ulrich Trautwein et al., "Between-Teacher Differences in Homework Assignments and the Development of Students' Homework Effort, Homework Emotions, and Achievement," *Journal of Educational Psychology* 101 (2009): 185.

5. Nancy E. Hill and Diana F. Tyson, "Parental Involvement in Middle School: A Meta-Analytic Assessment of the Strategies That Promote Achievement," *Developmental Psychology* 45 (2009): 740–63.

CHAPTER 27

Perfect, It Turns Out, Is What Practice Doesn't Make

We've long been eager to believe that mastery of a skill is primarily the result of how much effort one has put in. Extensive practice "is probably the most reasonable explanation we have today not only for success in any line, but even for genius," said the ur-behaviorist John B. Watson almost a century ago.

In the 1990s K. Anders Ericsson and a colleague at Florida State University reported data that seemed to confirm this view: What separates the expert from the amateur, a first-rate musician or chess player from a wannabe, isn't talent; it's thousands of hours of work.[1] (Malcolm Gladwell, drawing from but misrepresenting Ericsson's research—much to the latter's dismay—announced the magic number was ten thousand hours.)

It's daunting to imagine putting in that kind of commitment, but we're comforted nonetheless by the idea that practice is the primary contributor to excellence. That's true, I think, for three reasons:

1. *Common sense:* It seems obvious that the more time you spend trying to get better at something, the more proficient you'll become. That's why so many educators continue to invoke the old phrase "time on task," which, in turn, drives demands for longer school days or years and for more homework. Common sense, however, isn't always correct. Researchers have found that only when "achievement" is defined

---

"Perfect, It Turns Out, Is What Practice Doesn't Make" was originally published as a blog post on July 25, 2014.

as rote recall do we discover a strong, linear relationship with time. When the focus is on depth of understanding and sophisticated problem solving, time on task doesn't predict outcome very well at all—either in reading or math.[2]

2. **Protestant work ethic:** Many people simply don't like the idea that someone could succeed without having paid his or her dues—or, conversely, that lots of deliberate practice might prove fruitless. Either of these possibilities threatens people's belief in what social psychologists call a "just world." This sensibility helps to explain why copious homework continues to be assigned despite the lack of supporting data: We just don't want those kids goofing off, darn it—not in the evening and not even during the summer! Hence, too, the recent enthusiasm for "grit." (Interestingly, Ericsson collaborated with Angela Duckworth on that study of spelling bee champions described on pages 83–84.)

3. **Nurture over nature:** "Innate? Necessarily so!" is what we've heard for centuries. Given the tawdry history of biological reductionism, which usually manages to rationalize current arrangements of power as being due to the natural superiority of privileged groups, is it any wonder we remain leery of attributing success to inherited talent? It's more egalitarian to declare that geniuses are made, not born. Indeed, that skepticism is bolstered by evidence (from Carol Dweck and others) indicating that students are more likely to embrace learning if they believe their performance results from effort, something under their control, rather than from a fixed level of intelligence that they either possess or lack.

For many of us, then, Ericsson's conclusion has been deeply reassuring: Practice hard, and you'll do well. But along comes a meta-analysis, a statistical summary of 157 separate comparisons in 88 recent studies, that finds practice actually doesn't play nearly as significant a role as we'd like to think. "The evidence is quite clear that some people do reach an elite level of performance without copious practice, while other people fail to do so *despite* copious practice," wrote Brooke Macnamara and her colleagues.[3] In fact, they calculated that, overall, the amount of deliberate practice in which someone engages explains only 12 percent of the variance in the quality of performance. Which means 88 percent is explained by other factors.

But *what* other factors? It's common to assume that if practice matters less than we thought, then inborn ability matters more — as if there are only two contributors to excellence and they're reciprocally related. The *New York Times* headline for an article describing the new meta-analysis captured this assumption by reversing an old joke: "How Do You Get to Carnegie Hall? Talent."

That's not necessarily true, however. The question posed by Macnamara and her colleagues was appropriately open-ended: "We have empirical evidence that deliberate practice, while important, . . . does *not* largely account for individual differences in performance. The question now is what else matters." And there are many possible answers. One is how early in life you were introduced to the activity — which, as the researchers explain, appears to have effects that go beyond how many years of practice you booked. Others include how open you are to collaborating and learning from others, and how much you enjoy the activity.

That last one — intrinsic motivation — has a huge empirical base of support in workplaces, schools, and elsewhere. We've long known that the pleasure one takes from an activity is a powerful predictor of success. For example, one group of researchers tried to sort out the factors that helped third and fourth graders remember what they had been reading. They found that how interested the students were in the passage was *thirty times* more important than how "readable" the passage was.[4]

All of these factors overlap and serve as catalysts for one another, which means that even if practice does predict success to some degree, that doesn't mean it *caused* the success. Maybe the right question to ask is: Why do some people decide to practice a lot in the first place? Could it be because their first efforts proved mostly successful? That's a useful reminder to avoid romanticizing the benefits of failure. (See chapter 19.) Or, again, do they keep at it because they get a kick out of what they're doing? If that's true, then practice, at least to some extent, may be just a marker for motivation. Of course, natural ability probably plays a role in fostering both interest *and* success, and those two variables also affect each other.

But once we've introduced the possibility that interest plays an important role, we'd have to ask "Interest at what?" It doesn't make much sense to talk about the contribution of practice in the abstract. A lot depends on the task, among other things. Sure enough, Macnamara and her colleagues found, as is often the case with meta-analyses, that you can slice up the results by looking at an assortment of "moderator" variables — factors that affect the strength of the correlation between this and that.

For starters, the importance of practice depends on how investigators arrived at their figures for how much time people spent on their activities. Practice seemed to matter more in studies where the estimates were self-reported, as in Ericsson's original research with musicians. By contrast, when the hours were logged, and the estimates presumably more reliable, the impact of practice was much diminished. How much? It accounted for a scant 5 percent of the variance in performance. The better the study, in other words, the less of a difference practice made.[5]

Mostly, though, it depends on the domain. Practice explained 26 percent of the variance in achievement for games, 21 percent in musical accomplishment, 18 percent in sports, 4 percent in college grades, and less than 1 percent in professional success. What's true of time on task, then, is true of practice — which isn't surprising given how closely the two concepts are related. It depends on what you're doing. When the task is more complicated and open-ended, a lot of factors come into play that collectively swamp the effect of how much work you put in.

One last point. Even if Ericsson's conclusion, that expert-level performance can be explained primarily by thousands of hours of practice, had been supported rather than up-ended by this new review of research, it never had the relevance to education that some people have claimed. It never supported the value of giving students lots of practice problems. Why? First, because we can't simply assume that whatever promotes success in activities like music or chess also applies to, say, math or language arts.

Second, and more important, Ericsson was assessing the relative contribution of practice and talent. He didn't look at whether the teacher's goal was to reinforce an automatic response (borrow from the tens place, restate your conclusion in the last paragraph) as opposed to helping students make sense of ideas. In education — as opposed to, say, chess — everything depends on the kind of learning we want. Practice has much less of a role to play in promoting deep understanding than it does in expediting the memorization of algorithms or the reinforcement of behaviors. The Ericsson finding never really proved relevant to more meaningful learning, then — even back when that finding appeared to be true.

We may have to face the fact that our common-sense beliefs about excellence, or what we think *ought* to be the case about the importance of hard work, aren't necessarily true. But we can take comfort from knowing that less of a role for practice doesn't just mean that our destinies are fixed at birth.

NOTES

1. For example, see K. Anders Ericsson and Neil Charness, "Expert Performance: Its Structure and Acquisition," *American Psychologist*, August 1994: 725–47. Available at http://web.mit.edu/6.969/www/readings/expertise.pdf.

2. I reviewed research on "time on task" in *The Homework Myth* (Cambridge, MA: Da Capo Press, 2006), pp. 102–106. See www.alfiekohn.org/limits-time-task.

3. Brooke N. Macnamara, David Z. Hambrick, and Frederick L. Oswald, "Deliberate Practice and Performance in Music, Games, Sports, Education, and Professions: A Meta-Analysis," *Psychological Science* 25 (2014): 1608–18.

4. Richard C. Anderson et al., "Interestingness of Children's Reading Material," in *Aptitude, Learning, and Instruction, Vol. 3: Conative and Affective Process Analyses*, ed. Richard E. Snow and Marshall J. Farr (Hillsdale, NJ: Erlbaum, 1987). Also see Steven R. Asher, "Topic Interest and Children's Reading Comprehension," in *Theoretical Issues in Reading Comprehension: Perspectives from Cognitive Psychology, Linguistics, Artificial Intelligence, and Education*, ed. Rand J. Spiro et al. (Hillsdale, NJ: Erlbaum, 1980).

5. Something similar has been found with respect to claims about grade inflation, which usually turn out to be based on students' reports of their own grades. When we look at actual transcripts, it becomes much harder to defend the assertion that grades are higher now than they used to be, as Clifford Adelman discovered in extensive research he conducted for the U.S. Department of Education. See www2.ed.gov/rschstat/research/pubs/prinindicat/prinindicat.pdf.

PART 6

The Ends Behind

the Means

CHAPTER 28

Teaching Strategies That Work!
(Just Don't Ask "Work to Do What?")

So here's the dilemma for someone who writes about education: Certain critical cautions and principles need to be mentioned again and again because policy makers persist in ignoring them, yet faithful readers will eventually tire of the repetition.

Consider, for example, the reminder that schooling isn't necessarily better just because it's more "rigorous." Or that standardized test results are such a misleading indicator of teaching or learning that successful efforts to raise scores can actually lower the quality of students' education. Or that using rewards or punishments to control people inevitably backfires in multiple ways.

Even though these points have been made repeatedly (by me and many others) and supported by solid arguments and evidence, the violation of these principles remains at the core of the decades-old approach to education policy that still calls itself "reform." Hence the dilemma: Will explaining in yet another book, article, or blog post why its premises are dead wrong have any effect, other than to elicit grumbles that the author is starting to sound like a broken record?[1]

Another axiom that has been offered many times (but to no apparent effect) is that it means very little to say that a given intervention is "effective"—at least until we've asked "Effective at *what*?" and determined that the criterion in question is meaningful. Lots of educators cheerfully declare

"Teaching Strategies That Work! (Just Don't Ask 'Work to Do What?')" was originally published as a blog post on August 10, 2011.

that they don't care about theories; they just want something that works. But this begs the (unavoidably theoretical) question: What do you mean by "works"?

And once you've asked that, you're obligated to remain skeptical about simple-minded demands for evidence-, data-, or research-based policies. At its best, and on those relatively rare occasions when its results are clear-cut, research can only show us that doing A has a reasonably good chance of producing result B. It can't tell us whether B is a good idea, and we're less likely to talk about that if the details of B aren't even clearly spelled out.

To wit: There's long been evidence to demonstrate the effectiveness of certain classroom management strategies, most of which require the teacher to exercise firm control from the first day of school. But how many readers of this research, including teacher educators and their students, interrupt the lengthy discussion of those strategies to ask what exactly is meant by "effectiveness"?

The answer, it turns out, is generally some variation on compliance. If you do this, this, and this, you're more likely to get your kids to do whatever they're told. Make that explicit and you'd then have to ask whether that's really your paramount goal. If, on reflection, you decide that it's most important for students to become critical thinkers, enthusiastic learners, ethical decision-makers, or generous and responsible members of a democratic community, then the basic finding—and all the evidence behind it—is worth very little. Indeed, it may turn out that proven classroom management techniques *undermine* the realization of more ambitious goals because those goals call for a very different kind of classroom than the standard one, which is designed to elicit obedience.

An even more common example of this general point concerns academic outcomes. In scholarly journals, in the media's coverage of education, and in professional development workshops for teachers, any number of things are described as more or less beneficial—again, with scant attention paid to the outcome. The discussion about "promising results" (or their absence) is admirably precise about what produced them, while swiftly passing over the fact that those results consist of nothing more than scores on standardized tests, often norm-referenced and multiple-choice versions.

We're back, then, to one of those key principles, enunciated—and ignored—repeatedly: Standardized tests tend to measure what matters least about intellectual proficiency, so it makes absolutely no sense to judge curricula, teaching strategies, or the quality of educators or schools on the basis of the results of those tests. Indeed, as I've reported elsewhere,[2] test scores have actually been shown to be *inversely* related to deep thinking.

Thus, "evidence" may demonstrate beyond a doubt that a certain teaching strategy is effective, but it isn't until you remember to press for the working definition of effectiveness—which can take quite a bit of pressing when the answer isn't clearly specified—that you realize the teaching strategy (and all the impressive sounding data that support it) are worthless because there's no evidence that it improves *learning*. Just test scores.

Which leads me to a 2011 report in the *Journal of Educational Psychology*. A group of researchers at the City University of New York and Kingston University in London performed two meta-analyses, which is a way of statistically combining studies to quantify the overall result. The title of the article was "Does Discovery-Based Instruction Enhance Learning?," which is a question of interest to many of us.[3]

Would you like to know the much-simplified answer that the meta-analyzers reported? The first review, of 580 comparisons from 108 studies, showed that completely unassisted discovery learning is less effective than "explicit teaching methods." The second review, of 360 comparisons from 56 studies, showed that various "enhanced" forms of discovery learning work best of all.

There are many possible responses one might have to this news. One is "Duh." Another is "Tell me more about those enhanced forms, and which of them is most effective." Another is "Why did 108 groups of scholars bother to evaluate laissez-faire discovery given that, as these reviewers acknowledge, it constitutes something of a straw man since it's not the way most progressive and constructivist educators teach?" Yet another: "How much more effective are we talking about?" since a statistically significant difference can be functionally meaningless if the effect size is low.

But I took my own advice and asked *"What the hell did all those researchers, whose cooking was tossed into a single giant pot, mean by 'effective'?"* Pardon my italics, but it's astonishing how little this issue appeared to matter to the review's authors. There was no discussion of it in the article's lengthy introduction or in the concluding discussion section. Yes, "dependent variable" (D.V.) was one of the moderators employed to allow more specificity in crunching the results—along with age of the students, academic subject being taught, and so on. But D.V.—what discovery learning does or doesn't have an effect on—was broken down only by the type of measurement used in the studies: post-test scores vs. acquisition scores vs.

self-ratings. There wasn't a word to describe, let alone analyze, what all the researchers were looking for. Did they want to see how these different types of instruction affect kids' scores on tests of basic recall? Their ability to generalize principles to novel problems? Their creativity? (There's no point in wondering about the impact on kids' *interest* in learning; that almost never figures in these studies.)

Papers like this one are peer-reviewed and, as was the case here, are often sent back for revision based on reviewers' comments. Yet apparently no one thought to ask these authors to take a step back and consider what kind of educational outcomes are really at issue when different instructional strategies are compared. Never mind the possibility that explicit teaching might be much better than discovery learning . . . at producing results that don't matter worth a damn, intellectually speaking.

In fact, the D.V. in education studies is often quite superficial, consisting only of standardized test scores or a metric such as number of items taught that were correctly recalled. And if one of these studies makes it into the popular press, that fact about it probably won't. In chapter 23 I wrote about widespread media coverage of a study that supposedly proved one should, to quote the *New York Times* headline, "Take a Test to Really Learn, Research Suggests." Except that you had to read the study itself, and read it pretty carefully, to discover that "really learn" just meant "stuff more facts into short-term memory."

But the problem isn't just an over-reliance on outcome measures — rote recall, test scores, or obedience — that some of us regard as shrug-worthy and a distraction from the intellectual and moral characteristics that could be occupying us instead. The problem is that researchers are "burying the lede," as a journalist might put it. And too many educators don't seem to notice.

If this situation doesn't improve, please accept my apologies in advance because it's likely that I'll feel compelled to write another essay about it in the near future.

NOTES

1. In place of this dated simile, younger readers may substitute "like a corrupted music download."

2. Alfie Kohn, *The Case Against Standardized Testing* (Portsmouth, NH: Heinemann, 2000).

3. Louis Alfieri, Patricia J. Brooks, Naomi J. Aldrich, and Harriet R. Tenenbaum, "Does Discovery-Based Instruction Enhance Learning?" *Journal of Educational Psychology 103* (2011): 1–18.

CHAPTER 29

"Ready to Learn" Means Easier to Educate

The phrase "ready to learn," frequently applied to young children, is rather odd when you stop to think about it, because the implication is that some kids aren't. Have you ever met a child who wasn't ready to learn — or, for that matter, wasn't already learning like crazy? The term must mean something much more specific — namely, that some children aren't yet able (or willing) to learn *certain things* or learn them in a *certain way*.

Specifically, it seems to be code for "prepared for traditional instruction." And yes, we'd have to concede that some kids are not ready to memorize their letters, numbers, and colors, or to practice academic skills on command. In fact, some children continue to resist for years since they'd rather be doing other kinds of learning. Can you blame them?

Then there's the question of *when* we expect children to be ready. Even if we narrow the notion of readiness to the acquisition of "phonemic awareness" as a prerequisite to reading in kindergarten or first grade, the concept is still iffy, but for different reasons. For one thing, researcher Stephen Krashen points out that "about three-quarters of children who test low in P.A. [phonemic awareness] appear to have no serious problems in learning to read."[1] For another thing, the premise that one must be ready to start by a certain age is contradicted by evidence that children who don't learn to read until age seven or even later tend to make rapid progress and are soon indistinguishable from those who learned earlier.[2]

"'Ready to Learn' Means Easier to Educate" was originally published as a blog post on November 18, 2010.

Thus, "readiness to learn" may have more to do with a schedule that's convenient for others — or, worse, with preparation for standardized testing — than with what is necessary or even desirable for a given child. Perhaps the phrase is an attempt to put a positive spin on what is really just developmentally inappropriate practice. In any case, I fear the effect is to set up children (or their parents) for blame when certain goals aren't reached. "Well, what did you expect? This child arrived in our classroom *not ready to learn*."

Sometimes, though, readiness is invoked not as a justification for premature instruction but as a criterion for admission to a selective school or program. Only those certified as "ready to learn" are deemed eligible. For the moment, let's ignore the moral implications of making four- or five-year-olds compete for access to an elite educational setting. When the demand exceeds the (artificially scarce) supply, the decision is usually made to choose the most advanced children, the "smartest," the readiest.

But why?

Presumably because they will be the *easiest* to teach.

Martin Haberman, who coined the phrase "pedagogy of poverty," related a conversation he had with his grandson's kindergarten teacher at a selective school. "Wouldn't it make more sense to admit the children who *don't* know their shapes and colors, and teach them these things?" he asked. The teacher looked at him as if he were "leftover mashed potatoes," but he persisted:

> Next year my grandson, who is already testing in your top half, will have had the added benefit of being in your class for a whole year. Won't he learn a lot more and be even further ahead of the 4-year-olds who failed your admission exam and who have to spend this year at home, or in daycare, without the benefit of your kindergarten? Will the 4-year-old rejects ever catch up?

This question did even less to endear him to the teacher, but Haberman by now had realized what was going on more generally, and he summarized his epiphany as follows: "The children we teach best are those who need us least."[3]

As it happens, I had stumbled across this truth while thinking about education for a very different age group. Some years ago I was weighing the relative predictive power of high school grade-point average against that of the SAT or ACT. Some critics emphasize (correctly) that these exams are much less useful than grades at predicting college performance, but I was at pains to point out that grades have their own problems, and in any case it would be more sensible to lump them together into a compound variable called "gradesandtests," which fails to predict anything other than future gradesandtests; it tells us nothing about who will be creative or a deep thinker or excited about learning or happy or successful in his or her career.

But even this reframing of the discussion failed to challenge the premise that I, too, seemed to share with more conventional participants in the colloquy about college admission. The eminent psychologist David McClelland, known for his theory of achievement motivation, delivered a public lecture at the Educational Testing Service in 1971. This talk was devoted primarily to raising pointed questions about the value of intelligence tests (Do such tests predict "who will get ahead in a number of prestige jobs where credentials are important"? he asked rhetorically. Sure. And so does "white skin").

In an almost offhand way, McClelland then issued what struck me as a truly provocative and profound challenge. Why, he asked, do we spend time trying to figure out which criteria best predict success in higher education? Why are colleges looking for the most qualified students? "One would think that the purpose of education is precisely to improve the performance of those who are not doing very well," he mused. "If the colleges were interested in proving that they could educate people, high-scoring students might be poor bets because they would be less likely to show improvement in performance."[4]

Of course that's not how most colleges see the purpose of education. Like other institutions that get to choose whom to admit, they're looking for the applicants they think are ready to succeed. When you boil it down, that means excluding those who most need what they have to offer.

It's one thing to admit this guiltily, and something else again to build an admissions industry — from kindergarten to graduate school — around an unapologetic attempt to find the students who will be easiest to educate.

NOTES

1. Stephen Krashen, "Low P.A. Can Read O.K.," *Practically Primary 6* (2001): 17–20.

2. Stephen Krashen and Jeff McQuillan, "The Case for Late Intervention," *Educational Leadership*, October 2007: 68–73. Newer research confirms this: See Sebastian P. Suggate, Elizabeth A. Schaughency, and Elaine Reese, "Children

Learning to Read Later Catch Up to Children Reading Earlier," *Early Childhood Research Quarterly 28* (2013): 33–48.

3. Martin Haberman, *Star Teachers of Children in Poverty* (W. Lafayette, IN: Kappa Delta Pi, 1995), p. 80.

4. David C. McClelland, "Testing for Competence Rather Than for 'Intelligence,'" *American Psychologist*, January 1973: 6, 2.

CHAPTER 30

Just Another Brick in the Wall
How Education Researchers Ignore the Ends to Tweak the Means

"While we're at it, maybe we should just design classrooms without windows. And, hey, I'll bet kids would really perform better if they spent their days in isolation." My friend was reacting (facetiously, of course) to a new study that found kindergartners scored better on a test of recall if their classroom's walls were completely bare. A room filled with posters, maps, and the kids' own art constituted a "distraction."

The study, published in 2014 in *Psychological Science*,[1] was picked up by a number of media outlets even though it looked at a whopping total of twenty-four children. In the experiment, a research assistant read to these children about a topic such as plate tectonics or insects, then administered a paper-and-pencil test to see how many facts they remembered. On average, kids in the decorated rooms were "off task" 39 percent of the time and had a "learning score" of 42 percent. The respective numbers for those in the bare rooms were 28 percent and 55 percent.

Now if you regularly read education studies, you won't be surprised to learn that the authors of this one never questioned, or even bothered to defend, the value of the science lessons they used — whether they were developmentally appropriate or presented effectively, whether they involved anything more than reading a list of facts or were likely to hold any interest

---

"Just Another Brick in the Wall: How Education Researchers Ignore the Ends to Tweak the Means" was originally published as a blog post on June 4, 2014.

for five-year-olds. Nor did the researchers vouch for the quality of the assessment. Whatever raises kids' scores (on any test, and of any material) was simply assumed to be a good thing, and anything that lowers scores is bad.

Hence the authors' concern that children tend to be "distracted by the visual environment." Translation: They may attend to something in the room other than the facts an adult decided to transmit to them. And hence my friend's wry *reductio ad absurdum* response.

Alas, "sparse" classrooms had their own problems. There, we're told, children "were more likely to be distracted by themselves or by peers." Even if we strip everything off the walls, those pesky kids will still engage in instructionally useless behaviors like interacting with one another or thinking about things that interest them. The researchers referred to the latter phenomenon (thinking) as being "distracted by themselves." Mark that phrase as the latest illustration of the principle that, in the field of education, satire has become obsolete.

Our attention seems to be fixed relentlessly on the means by which to get students to accomplish something. As I pointed out in chapter 28, we remain undistracted by anything to do with ends—what it is they're supposed to accomplish and whether it's really valuable. Perhaps that's why schools of education typically require "methods" classes but not goals classes. In the latter, students might be invited to read this study and ask whether a child could reasonably regard the *lesson* as a distraction—from her desire to think, talk, or look at a cool drawing on the wall. Someone might insist that it's a teacher's job to decide what students ought to do and to maximize their "time on task." But such conversations—Time on *what* task? Why is it being taught? Who gets to decide?—are shut down before they begin when all we talk about (in schools of education, in journals, in professional development sessions) is how to maximize time on whatever is assigned.

Those of us who are disturbed, even outraged, by what's being done to our schools in the name of "reform" ought to consider how this agenda is quietly supported by research that relies on test scores as the primary, or even the sole, dependent variable. Then, too, there's the way such research is described by journalists. Most articles in *Education Week*, for example, ought to include this caveat:

> Please keep in mind that phrases such as "effective policies," "higher achievement," "better results," or "improved outcomes" refer only to scores on standardized tests. These tests are not only poor indicators

of meaningful intellectual accomplishment but tend to measure the socioeconomic status of the students or the amount of time they have been trained in test-taking skills.

The idea that kindergartners ought to block everything out but facts about plate tectonics reminded me of an essay called "Can Teachers Increase Students' Self-Control?" (as usual, the question was "can," not "should") written by a cognitive psychologist named Daniel Willingham. He offered as a role model a hypothetical child who looks through his classroom window and sees "construction workers pour[ing] cement for a sidewalk" but "manages to ignore this interesting scene and focus on his work."[2]

But what was the "work"? Was it a fill-in-the-blank waste-of-the-time that would lead any child to look out the window or at the wall? Or was it something so intellectually valuable that we'd be justified in saying, "Hey, this really is worthwhile"? I don't know. But for Willingham, as for so many others, it apparently doesn't matter: If the teacher assigned it, that's reason enough to ignore the interesting real-life lesson in how a sidewalk is created and to refrain from asking the teacher why that lesson can't be incorporated into the curriculum. An exemplary student is one who stifles his curiosity, exercises his self-control, and does what he's told.

I may not always be certain that a given lesson is worth teaching, but I'm pretty sure that's the question we should be asking—rather than employing discipline, or demanding self-discipline, or pulling stuff off the walls in order that students will devote their attention to something whose value is simply taken for granted.

NOTES

1. Anna V. Fisher, Karrie E. Godwin, and Howard Seltman, "Visual Environment, Attention Allocation, and Learning in Young Children: When Too Much of a Good Thing May Be Bad," *Psychological Science 25* (2014): 1362–70.

2. Daniel T. Willingham, "Can Teachers Increase Students' Self-Control?" *American Educator*, Summer 2011: 23. Also see my comments about the spelling bee study on pp. 83–84.

CHAPTER 31

What Parents Aren't Asked in School Surveys—and Why

The results of an opinion poll will vary—and not by a little—as a function of how the questions are phrased. "Do you favor special preferences for minorities in the form of affirmative action?" will attract many fewer favorable responses than "Do you favor efforts to help minorities get ahead in order to make up for past discrimination?" And then, of course, there are "push polls," which only pretend to sample people's views while attempting to influence them: "Would you be more or less likely to vote for Congressman McDoodle if you knew he was a practicing Satanist?"

I find myself thinking about how much more—and less—there is to polling than meets the eye whenever I come across one of those surveys that school administrators like to distribute to parents. I have to assume these are not intended as the equivalent of push polls, that there's a sincere desire to be responsive to the community and an honest pride in being able to cite "data" to judge the effectiveness, or at least the popularity, of school policies. (Data good.)

Too often, though, survey questions reflect a set of hidden assumptions about what's desirable, or inevitable. Moreover, they help to cement that view of education into place. The issues about which people are being asked to express their opinions are most revealing for what's not being asked: the underlying ideological commitments that aren't open to question. The more

---

"What Parents Aren't Asked in School Surveys—and Why" was originally published as a blog post on May 23, 2011.

we're asked to offer feedback about how well the school is doing *x*, the less apt we are to ask why *x* is being done in the first place, and what might be done instead.

Noam Chomsky put it this way:

> The smart way to keep people passive and obedient is to strictly limit the spectrum of acceptable opinion, but allow very lively debate within that spectrum—even encourage the more critical and dissident views. That gives people the sense that there's free thinking going on, while all the time the presuppositions of the system are being reinforced by the limits put on the range of the debate.[1]

So how does this play out in a school setting? Well, here's a question from a parent survey that someone forwarded to me from an Illinois elementary school: "Overall, the teaching (delivery of instruction) at _____ School is successfully preparing my child for his/her next academic level." (Strongly agree / agree / unsure / disagree / strongly disagree)

At least two premises inform this question, each of them a subliminal lesson for the parents who read it. The first is that teaching can be defined as the delivery of instruction. Students are the recipients of whatever is given to them, which means they are regarded—and expected to remain—fundamentally passive. Teachers, meanwhile, can be evaluated on the basis of how many facts or skills they have succeeded in delivering. When education is conceived this way, it would seem to follow that traditional methods of conveyance (lectures, worksheets, textbooks, etc.) and evaluation (tests and grades) are entirely appropriate. Indeed, their absence might even seem suspicious. If, instead, the parenthetical phrase in the survey question defined teaching as, say, "facilitation of active discovery of ideas," then parents might ask why their children were still being made to fill out worksheets or regurgitate answers on quizzes. But it doesn't. So they don't.

The second premise of this survey item is that what happens in each of the school's classrooms should be judged on the basis of how well it prepares kids for whatever is being done in other classrooms. Whether there's any merit, any intrinsic value, to those practices is apparently beside the point. Excluded from consideration are various other possible criteria, such as whether students are becoming more excited about learning, whether the curriculum is responsive to their interests and questions, and so on. (In fact, the particular school survey I've been reviewing includes a second question that asks whether parents believe the *curriculum*—as opposed to the teaching—is successfully preparing children for what comes next. Such repetition underscores the message that preparation is the point.)

I've written elsewhere about this rather curious rationale for subjecting younger children to dubious educational practices, including standardized testing, competition, grades, and homework. It doesn't matter that these things actually aren't beneficial, particularly for kids of this age. It doesn't even matter if they're downright harmful. All that counts is that people are going to subject children to these things later, so our obligation is to get them ready by doing these same things to them now. The survey in question not only fails to consider the implications of this rationale; it actively discourages such reflection by subtly communicating that the rationale is perfectly legitimate—indeed, a key criterion by which to evaluate teachers and schools.

Once you start noticing the implications of what's being asked, these parent surveys come to seem not merely less useful but positively insidious. You see a question about whether such-and-such is "promoting student success," and you wonder why there isn't a question about how the school is *defining* student success. Is it anything more meaningful than grades and test scores? Or you come across a survey item that asks you to agree or disagree with the statement "My child clearly understands school routines and expectations" (another actual question), and you want to replace it with: "Children are invited to participate in creating school routines and expectations rather than just doing what they're told."

You begin to suspect that parental feedback about issues like the latter is almost never sought in schools where there's little doubt about what the answer would be. (Parents might write in an option to the right of "strongly disagree" called "Ha!") And your stomach sinks as you anticipate the pride with which administrators will soon report that an overwhelming majority of our parents believe we're doing a damn fine job! Eighty-seven percent agree or strongly agree that we cram the facts into their children that the middle schools expect them to have been taught! Ninety-one percent report that their children can recite the prohibitions and punishments we've unilaterally devised and imposed on them! Is this a great school, or what?

———————

One of the topics about which parents seem to be surveyed with particular frequency is homework, and here we find a striking illustration of Chomsky's point about limiting meaningful discussion by eliciting opinions only within a narrow range. Probably the most common item—usually asked of parents rather than of the students themselves—is what might be called the Goldilocks question: "Do you think your child receives too much/too little/ about the right amount of homework?" The underlying assumption, of course, is that it's necessary to assign at least *some* homework. The question is designed to exclude critical responses to the whole concept.

One might be tempted, then, to right the balance by creating some mischievous alternative survey questions:

1. Given that research fails to find any benefit to homework for students who are younger than about fifteen, do you think they should be assigned homework anyway? Why?

2. Should children be required to devote their afternoons and evenings to academic tasks—even at the expense of their social, artistic, or physical development—or do you believe six or seven hours a day spent on such tasks is sufficient?

3. In your opinion, who should determine what happens during family time: the families themselves or the schools?

4. How likely do you think it is that homework will lead to optimal learning (and enthusiasm for learning) if all the students in a class— regardless of differences in their backgrounds, interests, and aptitudes—are required to complete the same assignment?

Too controversial? Maybe. But these questions are no more biased than the usual ones. It's just that the typical bias is harder to detect because it reflects and sustains the status quo. In any case, here are some questions that aren't loaded one way or the other and really ought to be asked:

- To what extent does your child's homework seem designed to deepen his or her understanding of important ideas? In your opinion, is it actually having that effect?

- Many educators and parents believe that the most important criterion by which school practices should be evaluated is whether they help children to become more excited about a given topic and about learning in general. Is the effect of your child's homework on his or her *desire* to learn generally positive, neutral, or negative?

- Do you think it makes more sense to assign homework on a regular basis or only when it's truly needed?

- Would you favor a voluntary system whereby families that want additional academic assignments after school could receive them, while families that would rather allow their children to pursue other activities could opt for no homework?

I don't know about you, but I don't think I've ever seen comparable questions about traditional education practices on a survey. Yet thinking about such practices and the values lurking behind them is exactly what parents and educators *should* be doing: not merely assessing how well the school is pursuing the agenda that's been set for it, but reconsidering the agenda itself—whom it benefits and whether it's consistent with our long-term hopes for our kids.

NOTE

1. Noam Chomsky, *The Common Good*. Interview by David Barsamian. Tucson, AZ: Odonian Press, 1998.

PART 7

Making Change

CHAPTER 32

Change by Decree

Everyone is opposed to making educators implement lousy ideas—
"lousy" being defined as something the speaker doesn't like. But it's a lot
more challenging to take a stand against—and, if you're in a position of relative power, to refuse to engage in—the practice of forcing educators to implement ideas you think are terrific.

In fact, we might say that true leaders are those who recognize that the
quality of an idea doesn't justify an attempt to shove it down people's
throats. Nor does it increase the likelihood that such an effort will be successfully digested. The idea will eventually just be, uh, coughed back up.

I've been collecting articles about educational administrators and other
officials who have tried to make various policy changes only to have their
heads handed to them. These changes include some I favor (replacing grades
with meaningful reports of student progress), some I oppose (defunding various programs to subsidize more on-line classes), and some about which I
have mixed feelings (shifting from lectures to guided discovery in an effort to
raise test scores). No doubt the affected teachers and parents had a range of
reactions to the substance of each proposal. But mostly they seem to have re-
sented change by decree.

Many of us have been appalled by the behaviorist, corporate-styled policies known collectively as "school reform." Its biggest proponents typically
don't know the first thing about pedagogy or assessment, so they rely on test
scores as a marker for improvement—even though schools may become
worse even as their scores climb. But what about educational theorists who

---

"Change by Decree" was originally published in American School Board Journal *in January 2013.*

know quite a bit about pedagogy and assessment—whose writings, in fact, eloquently explain the importance of having students construct ideas rather than passively absorb facts and skills—but who share with the clueless managerial types a belief that it's possible to improve by fiat what teachers do? Their assumption is that the best and brightest can (and should) reach into classrooms and *make* the instruction more thoughtful.

Consider the experts who have actively endorsed—not merely shrugged and passively accepted—the one-size-fits-all national Common Core "State" Standards. Their hope presumably was to use a project initiated by corporate executives, governors, and testing companies as a vehicle for improving teaching. But these experts may eventually reconsider—not only because of the nightmare of national testing that core standards will spawn, but because there will be massive (if passive) resistance from teachers. As there should be.

Beyond the moral objections, such efforts inevitably backfire. In the end, a policy maker or consultant cannot change what goes on in classrooms. All he or she can do is invite teachers to change what *they* do in class-rooms. To most teachers, it makes little difference if the marching orders come from the U.S. Department of Education or from the local school board. They're still orders. The model is still based on demanding ("Beginning next year . . .") rather than supporting ("What do you need? How can we help?"). Similarly, to parents in a given district, the question won't be whether a change announced by an administrator is sensible so much as whether they were consulted.

The paradox is almost painful when the new policy or program is about collaboration—say, an effort to create a sense of community in schools. (I'm less interested in number-crunching initiatives that cynically appropriate the *language* of "learning communities.") Three cheers when administrators want to shift their district's style from "doing to" to "working with." But that shift cannot itself be done *to* people.

When a mandate is handed down from the state capital, administrators and school board members, too, may be angry—particularly if it's idiotic, but even if it isn't. A leader's job then is to be a buffer, protecting those below them from the mandate's worst effects rather than robotically implementing and enforcing what doesn't make sense. But leaders should keep their initial irritation fresh in their minds in case they're ever tempted to imitate those who are higher up on the food chain by treating teachers the same way *they* were treated.

It's not just about "getting buy-in" for one's pet idea, a phrase that often comes across as patronizing because the focus is on strategies for deflecting resistance. True leaders are committed to a process that's genuinely respectful and collaborative, something closer to democratic decision-making from the beginning. If that's missing—if people are expected to get with the program just because they've been told it's good for kids—then administrators will be viewed with suspicion and their idea will never take root.

As the management theorist Peter Scholtes used to say, "People don't resist change. They resist being changed."

CHAPTER 33

Encouraging Courage

Education research doesn't always get the respect it deserves, but let's be honest: There's already enough of it to help us decide what to do (or stop doing) on many critical issues. Likewise, there are plenty of examples of outstanding classrooms and schools in which that research is being put into practice. What's lacking is sufficient courage for those examples to be widely followed.

It pains me to say this, but professionals in our field often seem content to work within the constraints of traditional policies and accepted assumptions — even when they don't make sense. Conversely, too many educators seem to have lost their capacity to be outraged by outrageous things. Handed foolish and destructive mandates, they respond only by requesting guidance on how to implement them. They fail to ask "Is this really in the best interest of our students?" or to object when the answer to that question is no.

The Cowardly Lion was able to admit that he lacked what made the muskrat guard his musk. Cowardly humans are more likely just to change the subject. Propose something that makes a meaningful difference, and you'll hear "But we've always . . . ," "But the parents will never . . . ," "But we can't be the only school in the area to . . ."

What, then, do truly courageous educators do? They dig deeper, they take responsibility, and they share power.

Digging Deeper. It requires gumption to follow one's principles wherever they lead. One may hope, for example, that children will be lifelong learners. One may even include that wish in a school's mission statement.

"Encouraging Courage" was originally published in Education Week *on September 18, 2013. This is a slightly expanded version of the published article.*

But what if evidence and experience tell us that interest in learning declines when students are graded and also when they're made to work on academic assignments after they get home from school? Are we willing to say, "If we're serious about our goals, then we must be willing to question any traditional practices — including grades and homework — that prevent us from reaching them"?

Advanced Placement courses often just accelerate the worst kind of lecture-based, textbook-oriented instruction. They're "rigorous," but that doesn't mean they're good. When it was reported that Scarsdale High School in New York joined other schools in deciding to drop all AP courses, an administrator at a nearby school circulated the article to his colleagues under the heading, "Do we have the guts?"

To dig deeper is to ask the root questions: not how *many* A.P. courses kids should take but whether to replace the College Board's curriculum with our own; not how *much* homework to assign but why kids should have to work a second shift every evening; not *how* to grade but whether to do so at all.

Even when practices seem to be producing good results, a courageous educator questions the criteria: "Wait a minute — we say this policy 'works,' but doesn't that just mean it raises scores on bad tests?" "My classroom may be quiet and orderly, but am I promoting intellectual and moral development, or merely compliance?" "We look good because our graduates get into prestigious colleges, but isn't that mostly because they come from affluent families? Are we helping them to become deep and passionate thinkers?"

Taking responsibility. The path of least resistance is to attribute problems to those who have less power than you. It's much harder to say, as a San Diego teacher did, "If a child starts to act up, I ask myself: 'How have I failed this child? What is it about this lesson that is leaving her outside the learning? How can I adapt my plan to engage this child?' I stopped blaming my children."

We have to be willing to take on the nay-sayers, to fight for what's right even in the face of concerted opposition. Maureen Downey, a reporter for the *Atlanta Journal-Constitution*, described how tough that can be in a culture where those "who speak up when they believe their students' welfare is at stake, and who question the system, earn the label of troublemaker." Lots of principals, she added, are "too cowed to practice 'creative insubordination.'"

Parting with power. It takes guts, not just talent, for a teacher to lead students beyond a predictable search for right answers — and to let them play an active role in the quest for meaning that replaces it. That entails not only accepting some unpredictability and messiness but also giving up some control.

A Washington teacher was proud of herself for having posted this sign at the front of her classroom: "Think for yourself; the teacher might be wrong!" But gradually she realized that her classroom wasn't really learner-centered. "I wanted [students] to think for themselves," she confessed, "but only so long as their thinking didn't slow down my predetermined lesson plan or get in the way of my teacher-led activity or argue against my classroom policies." It takes courage to admit one hasn't gone as far as one thought.

Over the years, I've met teachers who took a deep breath and let kids choose their own final grades, who tried out a no-homework policy to see what would happen, who stopped decorating the classroom by themselves and instead invited the kids to decide collectively how they wanted *their* classroom to look.

I've also met administrators who facilitated democratic decision-making among the staff instead of merely trying to get "buy in" to decisions they'd already made, who invited teachers to run the faculty meetings on a rotating basis rather than controlling all the meetings themselves (thereby modeling a top-down management style for teachers to reproduce in their classrooms), who suddenly realized that much of their airy talk about "responsibility," "citizenship," "character," and "motivation" really just amounted to euphemisms for obedience.

These days the greatest barrier to meaningful learning is the standards-and-testing juggernaut, the top-down, corporate-styled mandates that are squeezing the life out of classrooms. This, therefore, is where courage may be needed most desperately. I'm heartened by teachers — most recently in Seattle, but before them in Colorado, Massachusetts, and Illinois — who have refused on principle to administer standardized tests. ("How can I teach my kids to stand up for what they believe in if I'm not doing that myself?" asked one Chicago test boycotter.) And by hundreds of Florida teachers who tore up or returned their bonus checks for having produced high test scores (read: for having taught in a rich district). And by the New York superintendent who announced "it's time for civil disobedience" — and then worked to create an alternative diploma that wouldn't be based on high-stakes tests.[1]

I understand how real fear keeps more of us from doing what we know should be done. I don't want to blame the victims, or minimize the culpability of those who pass bad laws. But if every educator who understood the damage done by these policies decided to speak out, to organize, to resist, then the policies would soon collapse of their own weight. I often hear from teachers and administrators who debate whether to do so, who struggle with whether to teach in a way that responds to students' interests rather than follow a script or conform to prescriptive state (or national) standards. They know the risks but they also realize that Jonathan Kozol was right: "Abject capitulation to unconscionable dictates from incompetent or insecure superiors can be contagious."

It takes courage to stand up to absurdity when all around you people remain comfortably seated. But if we need one more reason to do the right thing, consider this: The kids are watching us, deciding how to live their lives in part by how we've chosen to live ours.

NOTE

1. For more examples, see Jesse Hagopian, ed., *More Than a Score: The New Uprising Against High-Stakes Testing* (Chicago: Haymarket Books, 2014).

Credits

Chapters described as blog posts appeared on the author's website as well as on some combination of the following three websites: the *Washington Post*'s "Answer Sheet" blog, the *Huffington Post*, and *Psychology Today*.

Chapter 1, "'We're Number Umpteenth!': The Myth of Lagging U.S. Schools" was originally published as a blog post on May 3, 2013.

Chapter 2, "Competitiveness vs. Excellence" was originally published as a blog post on August 9, 2010.

Chapter 3, "What Passes for School Reform: 'Value-Added' Teacher Evaluation and Other Absurdities" was originally published as a blog post on September 9, 2010.

Chapter 4, "STEM Sell: Do Math and Science Matter More Than Other Subjects?" was originally published as a blog post on February 16, 2011.

Chapter 5, "How to Sell Conservatism: Lesson 1 — Pretend You're a Reformer" was originally published as a blog post on October 20, 2010.

Chapter 6, "Operation Discourage Bright People from Wanting to Teach" was originally published as a blog post on November 1, 2010.

Chapter 7, "Remember When We Had High Standards? Neither Do I" was originally published as a blog post on December 10, 2010.

Chapter 8, "The Case Against Grades" was originally published in *Educational Leadership* in November 2011. This is a slightly expanded version of the published article.

Chapter 9, "Schooling Beyond Measure" was originally published in *Education Week* on September 19, 2012. This is a slightly expanded version of the published article.

Chapter 10, "Turning Children into Data: A Skeptic's Guide to Assessment Programs" was originally published in *Education Week* on August 25, 2010.

Chapter 11, "Whoever Said There's No Such Thing as a Stupid Question Never Looked Carefully at a Standardized Test" was originally published as a blog post on September 16, 2011.

Chapter 12, "Why the Best Teachers Don't Give Tests" was originally published as a blog post on October 31, 2014.

Chapter 13, "A Dozen Essential Guidelines for Educators" was originally published as a blog post on October 29, 2013.

Chapter 14, "What We Don't Know About Our Students — and Why" was originally published as a blog post on September 7, 2011.

Chapter 15, "The Trouble with Calls for Universal 'High-Quality' Pre-K" was originally published as a blog post on February 1, 2014.

Chapter 16, "Poor Teaching for Poor Children . . . in the Name of Reform" was originally published in *Education Week* on April 27, 2011. This is an expanded version of the published article.

Chapter 17, "Grit: A Skeptical Look at the Latest Educational Fad" was originally published in *Independent School* in Fall 2014. The article was adapted from

The Myth of the Spoiled Child: Challenging the Conventional Wisdom About Children and Parenting (Da Capo Press, 2014).

Chapter 18, "What Waiting for a Second Marshmallow *Doesn't* Prove" was originally published in *Education Week* on September 10, 2014. The article was adapted from *The Myth of the Spoiled Child: Challenging the Conventional Wisdom About Children and Parenting* (Da Capo Press, 2014).

Chapter 19, "What Do Kids Really Learn from Failure?" was originally published as a blog post on October 3, 2012.

Chapter 20, "Criticizing (Common Criticisms of) Praise" was originally published as a blog post on February 3, 2012.

Chapter 21, "Five Not-So-Obvious Propositions About Play" was originally published as a blog post on November 17, 2011. It was adapted from remarks delivered at the Coalition of Essential Schools Fall Forum in Providence, Rhode Island, on November 12, 2011.

Chapter 22, "Homework: An Unnecessary Evil?" was originally published as a blog post on November 26, 2012.

Chapter 23, "Do Tests Really Help Students Learn or Was a New Study Misreported?" was originally published as a blog post on January 28, 2011.

Chapter 24, "Studies Support Rewards and Traditional Teaching. Or Do They?" was originally published as a blog post on March 31, 2011.

Chapter 25, "Lowering the Temperature on Claims of Summer Learning Loss" was originally published as a blog post on July 20, 2012.

Chapter 26, "Is Parent Involvement in School Really Useful?" was originally published as a blog post on February 6, 2013.

Chapter 27, "Perfect, It Turns Out, Is What Practice Doesn't Make" was originally published as a blog post on July 25, 2014.

Chapter 28, "Teaching Strategies That Work! (Just Don't Ask 'Work to Do What?')" was originally published as a blog post on August 10, 2011.

Chapter 29, "'Ready to Learn' Means Easier to Educate" was originally published as a blog post on November 18, 2010.

Chapter 30, "Just Another Brick in the Wall: How Education Researchers Ignore the Ends to Tweak the Means" was originally published as a blog post on June 4, 2014.

Chapter 31, "What Parents Aren't Asked in School Surveys — and Why" was originally published as a blog post on May 23, 2011.

Chapter 32, "Change by Decree" was originally published in *American School Board Journal* in January 2013.

Chapter 33, "Encouraging Courage" was originally published in *Education Week* on September 18, 2013. This is a slightly expanded version of the published article.

INDEX

reading, *continued*

and race and class differences, 75, 120

and summer learning loss, 120

to children, 69–70

Reggio Emilia, 71, 76

research

brief vs. extended, 109–10n5, 115–18

misleading use of results from, 111–12

outcome measures in

lack of attention to, 136–37, 143–44

use of compliance as, 135

use of grades and tests as, 83–4, 94, 120–21, 126, 135–36

use of mechanical skills as, 108

use of rote recall as, 113, 137

rewards

for healthy lifestyles, 116–17

and school reform, 12

for teachers, 12, 53–4

verbal, 96–9

in the workplace, 117

Rich, Adrienne, 31

rigor, 40, 70, 75, 93, 100, 134, 156

Robbins, Jeff, 42–3

Rotberg, Iris, 4

Rothstein, Richard, 26, 31, 69–70

rubrics, 39, 49, 58

Ruopp, Faye, 56–7

S

Salzman, Harold, 19

Sartre, Jean-Paul, 21

Scholtes, Peter, 154

school "reform," 11–15

achieved by control of teachers, 26–8, 152–53

and conservatism, 23–5

effects of, on prospective teachers, 28–9

effects of, on style of teaching, 24–5, 76

goal of, 12, 27, 76, 152

media support for, 112

Schundler, Bret, 75

science. *See* STEM subjects

self-control, 80–6, 87–8, 90

self-discipline. *See* self-control

Seligman, Martin, 85

Sizer, Ted, 12, 61

Small Change, 66

Smith, Frank, 62n6

smoking cessation, 116–17

socioeconomic status. *See* poverty

spelling, 83–4, 128

Spencer, John, 44

V

"value-added" teacher evaluation, 13–14

W

Wassermann, Selma, 47

Watson, John B., 127

weight loss, 116–17

Willingham, Daniel, 145

willpower. *See* self-control

Wilson, Maja, 26–8, 58

Wrosch, Carsten, 82

Z

Zan, Betty, 71

Zhao, Yong, 5, 18–19